Workshop for Projects Management

ISBN: 978-1-326-16162-0

Copyright © Andreas Sofroniou, 2015

All rights reserved.

Copyright © Andreas Sofroniou 2015

Workshop for Projects Management

ISBN: 978-1-326-16162-0

*Andreas Sofroniou*

# 1. MANAGEMENT SUMMARY

## 1.1   Purpose of this Book

This book is intended to provide details and guidance on the Project/Programme Management Workshop.

The initiation of this document is based on requests for an objective tutorial and workshop for the Project Management community. A workshop package, which will serve as a helpful method for learning, practising and where possible interfacing with other courses.

The workshop material documented herewith will include the:

- Pre-workshop activities,
- Project Management principles,
- Integration of major methodologies,
- Case study details,
- Aid to participants' presentation,
- Established Project Management requirements,
- Interfaces of various tools,
- Referencing workshop material,
- Post-workshop coaching.

## 1.2 Use of the Document as a Manual

It is intended that this workshop manual will also assist those Programme/Project Managers who wish to use this document as a reference to other training packages.

The objective would be that, if a new, or existing Solution Centre wanted to roll out the workshop principles with minimal assistance, could just obtain the Programs Management Workshop package, point the candidates to the contents and guide them to the facilitators for any further training required.

The post-workshop idea of coaching, support, and mentoring for the Programme/Project Managers will be continued.  Thus, the Solution Centre will be able to call as and when help is needed.

## 1.3 Alterations and Distribution

The distribution of this initial study will be restricted to the members of the team, only. Please note that the contents of this document may have to be altered, prior to any subsequent distribution/s, outside the prescribed course.

## 2. PRE-WORKSHOP ACTIVITIES

### 2.1 Case Study

As a preparation, prior to the workshop, the participants will be supplied with the précis of a Case Study. The case study chosen for the workshop should be based on an existing project, or one currently being developed.

In order to familiarise the reader, an abstract is to be shown before the workshop commences. Remembering that the implementation of a time critical project requires a large number of soft skills, in addition to the standard set of project management hard skills and supporting toolsets in order to ensure a successful delivery on time and within budget.

This paper will provide a case study of how a successful collaboration is achieved between two distinct organisations. In working together, they delivered a time-critical project and implemented a major change to the format.

The following topics of interest to project managers to be covered in this paper:

1. Establishment of ground rules for the engagement and the 'modus operandi',

2. Determination of requirements process - soft skills required,

3. Team empowerment and skill sets and how this fits into a structured project management environment,

4. How the project managers of each organisation adopted an empowering and collaborative management style,

5. Internal and external issues that had to be overcome in adopting this collaborative approach,

6. How the project managers knew if they had been successful in meeting the objectives of both organisations - the mechanisms that existed for formal and informal reviews.

The candidate's assessment of the case study will be based on the Project Score Card Questionnaire, of which a summary is shown below.

## 2.2 Assessment

| PMI Key Area | Workshop Module | Functional Skills Workshop 2 for PPMJF Level 3-4 staff | Self-assessment Pre-Workshop ABCD (A=Excellent D=Poor) | Self-assessment During Workshop ABCD (A=Excellent D=Poor) | Self-assessment End of Coaching ABCD (A=Excellent D=Poor) |
|---|---|---|---|---|---|
| 1. Integration Management | | | | | |
| 2. Scope Management | | | | | |
| 3. Time Management | | | | | |
| 4. Cost Management | | | | | |

| PMI Key Area | Workshop Module | Functional Skills Workshop 2 for PPMJF Level 3-4 staff | Self-assessment Pre-Workshop ABCD (A=Excellent D=Poor) | Self-assessment During Workshop ABCD (A=Excellent D=Poor) | Self-assessment End of Coaching ABCD (A=Excellent D=Poor) |
|---|---|---|---|---|---|
| 5. Quality Management | | | | | |
| 6. Human Resource Management | | | | | |
| 7. Communications Management | | | | | |
| 8. Risk Management | | | | | |
| 9. Procurement Management | | | | | |
| 10. Other | | | | | |

## 2.3 The Main Headings of the Score Card.

This questionnaire is based on practical experience, gained from a large number of projects in the Information Technology industry. It should be used throughout the project lifecycle.

| Topic Area | Value | True ? (Y/N) | Points | Topic Area | True ? Y/N) |
|---|---|---|---|---|---|
| | | | | 6 PROJECT | |
| 1 USER PARTICIPATION | 17.5 | | | PLANNING 10 | |
| 2 REQUIREMENTS | | | | 7 RISK | |
| MANAGEMENT | 17.5 | | | MANAGEMENT .5 | |
| | | | | 8 TECHNICAL | |
| 3 COMMUNICATION | 15 | | | ENVIRONMENT 5 | |
| | | | | 9 QUALITY | |
| 4 BUSINESS ORIENTATION | 12.5 | | | MANAGEMENT 5 | |
| 5 PROJECT TEAM | 10 | | | | |

*OVERALL PROJECT STATUS:*     Green: 80-100

Amber:61-79.5

Red: 0-60.5

TOTAL PROJECT SUCCESS
POTENTIAL (0-100)

## 2.4 Main Points of the Programme Management Key Areas

- INTEGRATION

- SCOPE

- TIME

- COST

- QUALITY

- HUMAN RESOURCE

- COMMUNICATION

- RISK

- PROCUREMENT

# 3  THE MODEL AND LINES OF BUSINESS

## 3.1  Business Model

A Business Model ensures clients receive superior service execution.  We go to market through five global lines of business (LOBs), which are co-ordinated at the account level through our Client Executive (CE) organisation.  This mix of global capabilities and a focus on service excellence at the client level will enable the company to become the "leader in the Digital Economy."

## 3.2 Strategy

In general terms, the corporate strategy is to leverage our capabilities and resources across five lines of business (LOBs).  We go to market through these five global businesses, co-ordinated at the account level through our Client Executive (CE) organization.  This mix of global capabilities and a focus on service excellence at the client level enables the company to become the "leader in the Digital Economy."

## 3.3 Strategy Overview

Company 'A' - Provides a full spectrum of management consulting capabilities including strategy, operations and information technology services; builds Digital Economy consulting leadership by extending core services and collaborating to deliver end-to-end value.

Company 'B' - Helps clients achieve superior value in the Digital Economy by aligning the right people and integrating the right processes; focuses on growth by bringing new capabilities to market, increased account penetration and improved service excellence.

E Solutions - Combines diverse electronic business and solutions consulting offerings into a single organization; creates a bridge between value-added management consulting and information technology (IT) outsourcing and Business Process Management (BPM); shift to global consulting model while dominating select Digital Economy markets.

Information Solutions - Integrates innovative technology with business strategy to produce solutions that:

1) Meet specific client IT needs,

2) Address mission-critical business issues and

3) Support our clients' desired place in the turbulent e-market-space; pursues high-growth opportunities and expands market reach.

Overall Solutions - Provide software products and services to customers seeking to integrate their customer and supplier strategies with product development, manufacturing and service strategies. Also, aim to be the defining entity for product lifecycle solutions for virtual enterprises.

# 4. INTERFACING

## 4.1 The Diagrammatic Representation of the Desired Integration

The diagrammatic flow shown below is the desired overall integration of related top-level processes:

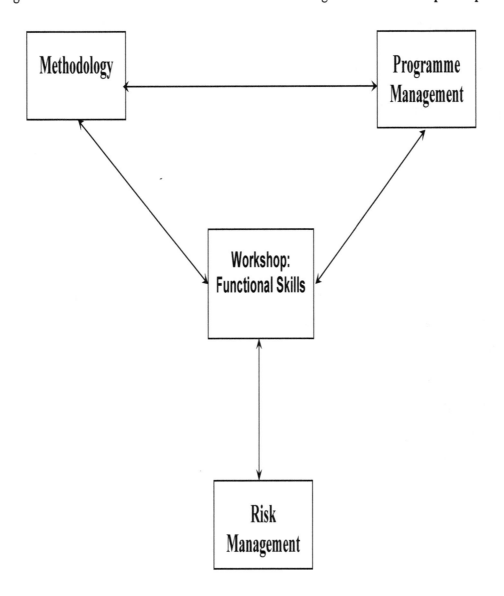

## 4.2 Using the Existing Methods

In interfacing the various processes from the different existing methodologies the main steps of Projects/Programme Management will be incorporated in this exercise.

### 4.2.1 The main six stages of system development:

- Define,

- Analyse,

- Design,

- Construct,

- Optimise,

- Implement.

### 4.2.2 Programme Management: The four main stages of:

- Start-up,

- Planning,

- Execution,

- Closedown.

### 4.2.3 Risk Management: The four main processes of:

- Issues,

- Assumptions,

- Risks,

- Plans.

## 4.3 Tools Interfaces

The tools shown above and their functional listing have a dual purpose:

- Enable the workshop participant/reader to obtain the necessary references/material for their workshop presentations.

- Show the various processes and functions.

The actual points of interfacing the various stages of development, the procedures of managing projects and the assumptions analysis of the methodology, are explored in the workshop and in this document.

Subsequent to the three-day workshop, the 'coaching/mentoring' period will include a pilot practice of the courseware, locally. Further on, it is suggested that the participants evaluate the success of the rollout. Should the rollout be successful, then gain approval for widespread adoption. Thereafter, adjust the practice and courseware for global use and make the practice and courseware available (curriculum update) across the organisation.

## 4.4 Progressive Steps

For the Workshop: Functional Skills to achieve a global acceptance some broader issues need to be resolved. Since a company's training policy is to train only global processes, and the selected Project Managers Workshop: Functional Skills is not yet a truly global process, Programme/Project Management Community Leadership need to plan around that.

As such, this study is considering various progressive steps, some of which are in the process of being completed. The following have taken into consideration:

1. The Workshop: Functional Skills Practice roll out to be compliant with an agreed method.

2. Subsequently, or whenever possible in parallel, organisation' training establishment to review the Workshop: Functional Skills courseware

and decide what needs to be done to render it training-compliant.

3. A director's level individual will decide when the rollout is successful, and accordingly recommend the workshop as a global process. If accepted, the Programme/Project Management Community Leadership will align the workshop to the global preferred process.

Regarding the rollout of the Workshop training, various departments need to identify the target audience, and recommend candidates for this type of training.

# 5. FUNCTIONAL SKILLS

## 5.1 Filling the Gap

There can be little doubt that Project Management will become increasingly important in the years ahead for any organisation. This workshop is, therefore, aiming to fill a gap in the current business and tutorial literature.

## 5.2 Programme Management Overview

This Workshop has been designed for the Programme/Project Manager and the computer professional who needs an overview of Project Management.

The Workshop deals with the Management of Projects, where established management procedures and various development methods are explained.

This Workshop is intended to give Project Management staff an overview of the Project Development Methods and some indication of how these relate to the various Project Management Techniques.

## 5.3 The Fundamentals

The Workshop explores the fundamental aspects of operational computing and the development of new information systems. Projects are conceived and grow from a business need, but what seems clear at the beginning often becomes blurred and confused.

In the end projects may not deliver what was expected and costly investment produces few benefits. The Project Management case study described in this workshop provides a generic model product breakdown structure for an IT system down to the third level, which gives a starting point for project-specific planning.

## 5.4 Standards

Just as architects need sets of standards to help them with their plans, so do Systems Analysts, Designers, and Programmers. The Project Management and Development Methods described in this book are such, a set of standards.

The book contains certain rules, which can be used to develop systems. They are not a substitute for training and experience but a support for these.

The methods must be applied with experience and common sense in different ways to different projects. Only well-trained professionals can do this.

In preparing this workshop, the facilitator is mostly concerned with the development and the managing of systems and people in all types of companies, the multi-national corporations, as well as their dedicated divisions.

# 6. MANAGEMENT FUNCTIONS

## 6.1 Introduction to Management Functions

The most important functions that top executives perform include setting policies, planning, and preparing budgets. At the strategic level, these decision-making functions are supported by executive information systems. The objective of these systems is to gather, analyse, and integrate internal (corporate) and external (public) data into dynamic profiles of key corporate indicators.

Depending on the nature of the business, such indicators may relate to the status of high-priority programmes, health of the economy, inventory, and cash levels, performance of financial markets, relevant efforts of competitors, utilisation of manpower, legislative events, and so forth.

The indicators are displayed as text, tables, graphics, or time series, and optional access is provided to more detailed data. The data emanate not only from within the company's production and administrative departments but also from global information sources.

## 6.2 Ideal and Real World of Information Systems

The present-day efforts are to enhance Project Management information systems with adaptive and self-organising abilities by means of learning from the Project Managers' changing information needs and uses.

THE REAL WORLD OF PROJECT MANAGEMENT

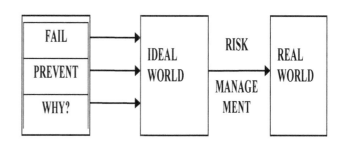

The Project Management systems make use of computational aids for data classification, modelling, and simulation.

Because of the enormous complexity of typical Project Management responsibilities, the number of changes that can be made and the alternatives that can be pursued, a productive body of quantitative methods has been developed to solve project management problems.

Administrative functions in multi-national organisations have as their objective the husbanding and optimisation of corporate resources - namely, employees and their activities, inventories of materials and equipment, facilities, and finances.

The global administrative information systems support this objective. They focus primarily on resource administration and provide project management with reports of aggregate data.

Executive information systems may be viewed as an evolution of administrative information systems in the direction of strategic tracking, modelling, and decision-making.

Functionally close to payroll systems are personnel information systems, which support the administration of the organisation's human resources.

Job and salary histories, inventory of skills, performance reviews, and other types of personnel data are combined in the database to assist personnel administration, explore potential effects of reorganisation or new salary scales (or changes in benefits), and match job requirements with skills.

Project management information systems concentrate on resource allocation and task completion of organised activities.

6.3 Project Management and Planning Techniques

Project managers frequently face the task of controlling projects that contain unknown and unpredictable factors. When the projects are not complex, bar charts can be used to plan and control project activities.

These charts divide the project into discrete activities or tasks and analyse each task individually to indicate weekly manpower requirements. As the work goes forward, progress is charted and estimates are made on the effects of any delays or difficulties encountered during the completion of the project.

A successful corporation is introducing more sophisticated methods of project planning and control on an ongoing basis. Variations and extensions of techniques are now in use, and they have proven particularly valuable for projects requiring the co-ordinated work of employees and contractors. Project planning and control techniques are now common in many client environments.

In actual projects the relationships among the required tasks are often complex. In many companies efforts to improve existing products and processes have been formalised.

## 6.4 Managing Projects

Business organisations often have problems in deciding and it is very easy to take a narrow view. For example, many people believe that a project must involve computers in some way. However, a much broader view is required when the following definition is considered.

*"A project is a management environment, set up to deliver a business product to a specified business case."*

In other words, a project is temporary with a temporary organisation, which only exists to deliver something (a product) that is considered worthwhile to the business. This temporary situation has two important characteristics. It is a one-off and it is introducing change via the delivered products.

Project products are wide-ranging and diverse in their scope. The resulting product may be a bridge, a road, the procurement of equipment, restructuring an organisation, relocating an office, or a computer system. The environment created and the work done to deliver the product is a project.

Projects are conceived and grow from a business need, but what seems clear at the beginning often becomes blurred and confused. In the end projects may not deliver what was expected and costly investment produces few benefits.

It is little wonder that things go wrong and projects fail, not because people are ineffective, but because of the sheer complexity of project management. A recent UK statistical survey found that 80% of the reasons for project failure were management, not technical.

Some of the problems may be familiar to project managers at all levels:

1. No standard approach to project management,

2. Lack of communication between client users and project management, of project requirements, of accurate and realistic progress

information, of clear responsibilities for line and project management,

3. Inadequate planning and controls,

4. Inadequate Business Case to justify the project,

5. Unclear project definition, objectives and scope,

6. Uncontrolled change,

7. Skills shortage of experienced project managers,

8. Inadequate team building and staff motivation,

9. Taking uncontrolled shortcuts, due to (perceived) lack of time,

10. Inadequate documentation,

11. Lack of commitment,

12. Inadequate quality standards.

## 6.5 Solutions

Unlike line management, which deals with operational issues and maintaining existing services, project management deals with the unprecedented, the unfamiliar, and the need for change.

Over the years it has become recognised that there is a common thread running through the management of projects. Much of this is common sense and it was the formalisation of this common sense, plus traditional management good practice, into a structure, which gave rise to project management methods.

The main characteristics of a near enough efficient Programme/Project Management may include:

- Decision making,

- Information gathering,

- Relating to others,

- Dealing with change,

- Stress management,

- Handling of conflicts,

- Work planning,

- Managing risks,

- Motivation and Persuasion

- Delivery.

There are many project management methods available, each of which is characterised by the way in which it provides principles, procedures, and techniques for the management of projects. Methods utilise existing standard techniques as well as introducing their own unique features.

It is probably impossible for all projects to succeed, but the number of project failures can be dramatically reduced by the proper application of a structured project management method.

Such methods include Structures Systems Analysis and Designing, Programme Management tools. Risk Management and Change Management.

The author has already published books for all the methods mentioned in the above sentence. All provide project management principles and processes to address the problems mentioned earlier.

# 7. PROJECT MANAGEMENT AND THE POST-WORKSHOP COACHING AND MENTORING

## 7.1 Project Management (PM), a Profession

Project Management is actually a profession rather than an industry. For each project that the Project Manager is responsible for, he or she will be involved in a range of tasks that tend to start with the initial clarification of the project's objectives, scope, constraints and reporting rules.

Through initiation activities, identifying all the actions that are involved in the project, estimating the duration of individual tasks, looking at the dependency one activity has on another and calculating the critical path/s in the project where any slippage will cause delays to the end date.

It is, therefore, vital that Project Managers undertake a level of training that will introduce them to the skills and attributes that are needed in the role. Further on, today organisations demand high quality, suitably qualified Project Managers in most projects.

## 7.2 Post-workshop Coaching and Mentoring

Because of such demands, the Workshop has been designed with emphasis on the post-workshop coaching and mentoring.

Coaching is about transforming the Project Manager's possibilities for the future. It is about how a Project Manager can significantly speed up his/her professional and personal continuous development, to get the results he/she wants in all areas of the programme/project/s.

So coaching gives the Project Manager the opportunity to focus on her/his needs, which in turn enable the Project Manager to concentrate on the business at hand. Working with a coach/mentor, after the actual workshop, gives the Project Manager the opportunity to be exceptional at what she/he does.

The Project Manager wants results quickly. The post-workshop coaching can speedily get focused and identify the participant's own individual needs. This relationship between the participating Project

Manager and the facilitating coach/mentor has to be built on trust, confidentiality, and mutual respect.

## 7.3 The Interpersonal Skills of the Coach

The participating Project Manager should expect the coach/mentor to have excellent interpersonal skills so that the Project Manager feels relaxed, comfortable and prepared to trust the feedback. Of paramount importance is the ability of the coach/mentor to be an empathetic listener.

The Project Manager is, also, looking for someone who has a sound background in general business and management. A coach, who will be able to understand the kind of issues that a Project Manager may be facing; whilst the mentor may not already be familiar with the project, he/she needs to quickly get to know the Project Manager's business and project/s.

The Project Manager participating in the workshop must meet the potential coach and then decide how well they relate to each other. The Project Manager can then decide whether she/he wants a single coaching session or an ongoing month-long

relationship. The Project Manager can use the mentor/coach to help him/her deal with specific business or personal issue, to develop particular interpersonal skills, or simply as a sounding board.

The candidate of the workshop may discover that the post-workshop mentoring is such a rewarding experience, that the Project Manager may wonder how he/she ever did without it!

# 8. THE BENEFITS OF PROJECT MANAGEMENT

Actual users have attributed the summarised main benefits listed below to Project Management.

1. Provides the basis for controlling the implementation of strategic business plans.

2. Promotes the business view for the justification of projects and provides mechanisms for ensuring their ongoing viability and business integrity.

3. The organisation structure encourages user and business participation at all levels and can be tailored to any type, size and complexity of project.

4. Separates and clearly identifies and defines, the roles and responsibilities in project management.

5. The stage concept provides the basis for conscious and continuous management control.

6. Concentrates on the real goals of the project, through the products, to ensure a common understanding about what is being produced.

This product orientation also enables better estimating, planning, and control.

7. The planning and control mechanisms are tailored and structured to one another.

8. Quality is planned, controlled and assured from the outset of the project.

9. Provides an excellent vehicle for encouraging the right people to make the right decision at the right time.

10. Confronts the management of risk and uncertainty by asking questions and forcing issues into the open. Dealing with issues can reduce project costs before they become problems.

11. Simplifies paperwork by concentrating on essential documentation and the provision of simple but effective reporting procedures.

# 9. WORKSHOP AGENDA

## 9.1 Workshop Name

| Version | Modified By | Date | Approved by | Approval Date | Revisions |
|---------|-------------|------|-------------|---------------|-----------|
|         |             |      |             |               | For comments |
|         |             |      |             |               | Initial document |
|         |             |      |             |               | Workshop Structure & timing |
|         |             |      |             |               | • Include few comments in yellow<br><br>• Agenda<br><br>• Could be a generic structure for a whole Workshop<br><br>• Parts of the agenda might be used for each module. |

## 9.2 Workshop (WS) Timetable

| Time Table | Topics | Method and Goals | Material/s | Who |
|---|---|---|---|---|
| *1.1 DAY ONE*<br><br>1.2 Session starts at *09.00* | Opening of workshop and welcoming of participants. | Introduction by workshop deliverer | None | Workshop deliverer |
| 12 participants x 2 minutes each = 24 minutes<br><br>*10.30 – 11.00* | Participants getting acquainted. | Salutations and introductory activities | None | Participants |
| 60 minutes<br><br>*11.00 – 12.00* | • Objectives of WS and the Curriculum<br><br>• WS ground rules<br><br>• Agenda and WS structure<br><br>• Scope of WS | • Presentation of topics to group,<br><br>• Consensus on WS rules,<br><br>• Presentation of agenda, | Presentation displayed via beamer<br><br><br>Pin-boards, pins, pens, cards and labels | WS deliverer |

| Time Table | Topics | Method and Goals | Material/s | Who |
|------------|--------|------------------|------------|-----|
| | | • Presentation of topics which can be addressed in WS,<br><br>• Address problems. (Individual problems will be discussed in depth during coaching session),<br><br>• Mapping of individual issues to WS issues,<br><br>• Placement.<br><br>• Charts displayed in room during | Usual facilitation material & accessories<br><br>Confidentiality | |

| Time Table | Topics | Method and Goals | Material/s | Who |
|---|---|---|---|---|
| | | WS,<br><br>• Agenda displayed in room to mark progress.<br><br>• Verbal explanation of WS | | |
| **45 minutes**<br>*12.00 – 12.45* | **BREAK for LUNCH** | | | |
| 60 minutes<br><br>*12.45 - 13.45* | Participants' expectations & goals.<br><br>Facilitated discussion of completed pre-activities. | Facilitate discussion of WS group.<br><br>The following questions and points are used as a guidance for the participants: | Have the points listed on flipchart, whiteboard, or displayed via beamer<br><br>Make use of the Key Areas, as an auxiliary aid to the | WS deliverer steering the discussion.<br><br>WS participants to discuss. |

| Time Table | Topics | Method and Goals | Material/s | Who |
|---|---|---|---|---|
| | | • What do you want to get out of this WS?<br><br>• List your 3 main goals.<br><br>• In which area would you like to enhance you knowledge?<br><br>• List areas where you would like to be supported during coaching period.<br><br>• List most critical issue in a current project. | discussion<br><br>Utilise the Score Card, as an example on how to review the WS case study and projects in general | |

| Time Table | Topics | Method and Goals | Material/s | Who |
|---|---|---|---|---|
| | | • What prevents your project from being successful? <br><br> • What will make your project successful? | | |
| 15 minutes <br><br> *13.45 – 14.00* | Sum up of major points requiring further attention | List the most important thing/s, lesson/s learned and tool/s to be shared among candidates. | Flipcharts/whiteboard | Candidates |
| 60 minutes <br><br> *14.00 – 15.00* | Integrated Methodologies. <br><br><br> Introduction to Project Management | Project Management methodology, Risk & Change Management, Structured Analysis/Designing. <br><br> Integration of Methodologies. | Displayed via beamer. | WS Deliverer. |

| Time Table | Topics | Method and Goals | Material/s | Who |
|---|---|---|---|---|
| | | Project Management principles. | | |
| 15 minutes *15.00 –15.15* | **Mid-afternoon break** | | | |
| 60 minutes *15.15 – 16.15* | **Mapping of participants' individual expectations (pre-activities) to WS issues (matrix).** | Grouping of top 3 expectations and/or issues on Pin-board. (To be prepared by WS Deliverer.)  Participants to write issues, problems, observations down on cards and pin them on pin-board in the respective area of matrix: | Group activity.  Pin-board with prepared matrix. | Participants to classify.  WS Deliverer to facilitate. |

| Time Table | Topics | Method and Goals | Material/s | Who |
|---|---|---|---|---|
| | | • Identification of Issues, | | |
| | | • Writing issues and problems on cards. | | |
| | | • Grouping of cards into predefined headings, based on the PMI key areas. | | |
| | | • Reviewing of cards with group, | | |
| | | • Clarification where applicable, | | |
| | | • Identification of duplicated points | | |

| Time Table | Topics | Method and Goals | Material/s | Who |
|---|---|---|---|---|
| | | and re-group were applicable. | | |
| 60 minutes<br><br>*16.15 – 17.15* | Case Study Review<br><br>Part 1<br><br>Create collection of the issues and problems, which the participants identified in the case study during the pre-WS preparation.<br><br>State what individual issues/problems will be addressed. | Participants to write issues, problems, observations down on cards and pin them on pin-board under the respective heading:<br><br>Identification of Issue<br><br>Writing issues & problems on cards<br><br>Grouping of cards into predefined headings based on the key areas. | Use of to be developed Case Study<br><br>Pin board<br><br>Defined headings to group issues. | WS deliver facilitate<br><br>WS participants input their findings |

| Time Table | Topics | Method and Goals | Material/s | Who |
|---|---|---|---|---|
| | | Review of cards with group: <br> • Clarify where applicable, <br> • Eliminate doubles, <br> • Re-group were applicable. | | |
| DAY TWO <br> 15 minutes <br> *09:00–0 9:15* | Recap of day 1 | Presentation | Displayed via beamer with reference to wall material | WS Deliverer |
| 60 minutes <br><br> *09.15 – 10.15* | Case Study Review <br><br> Part 2 <br><br> Add individual project issues etc. to collection of case study issues. | Review the personal issues and problems the participants provided during 'Participants expectations & goals' topic. | Pin board <br><br> Defined headings to group issues. | WS deliverer |

| Time Table | Topics | Method and Goals | Material/s | Who |
|---|---|---|---|---|
| | | Add them to the collection of issues & problems identified in the case study where applicable.<br><br>Doing so, will address some of the identified issues and problems.<br><br>Solutions and recommendations will follow, during the workgroup session. | | |
| **15 minutes**<br>*10.15 – 10.30* | **Mid-morning Break** | | | |
| 60 minutes<br><br>*10.30 – 11.30* | Case Study Review<br><br>Re-group candidates | At beginning of WS each participant is provided with an | Prepared envelopes, Number of areas are distributed equally | WS deliverer to ask every participant at beginning of WS to |

| Time Table | Topics | Method and Goals | Material/s | Who |
|---|---|---|---|---|
| | into workgroups | envelope, which states a problem, based on WS module, functional skills, and any other key areas.<br><br>The content of the envelope to be grouped with the persons that have the same area stated on their cards. | to the number of participants | draw one envelope |
| 60 minutes<br><br>*11.30 – 12.30* | Case Study Review<br><br>Plan session<br><br>Each workgroup to be presented with one problem area, the associated issues and problems | Each Workgroup to identify:<br><br>• Root cause/underlying problem, Recommendation on how to fix it, Define | • Define time allowed for exercise<br><br>• Separate groups within meeting room<br><br>• Flipchart paper, | Individual workgroups<br><br>WS deliverer to interact with groups to track progress and help where appropriate |

| Time Table | Topics | Method and Goals | Material/s | Who |
|---|---|---|---|---|
| | | solution.<br>• Input: issues collection<br><br>• Process: Participants use flipchart of slides to collect their findings.<br><br>• Media is used to present findings and recommendations to large groups<br><br>• Output: recommendations to solve issues – of case study, and for the | pens<br><br>• Allocate timescales for presentations, for each group<br><br>• Define template of points to be addressed during presentation, based on root cause, alternative way to resolve issue and recommendation. | |

| Time Table | Topics | Method and Goals | Material/s | Who |
|---|---|---|---|---|
|  |  | raised issues of the individuals |  |  |
| 45 minutes<br>*12:30 – 13.15* | BREAK for LUNCH |  |  |  |
| 60 minutes<br><br>*13.15 – 14.15* | Case Study Review<br><br>Presentations of Workgroup results | Root causes and resolutions proposal to be presented by workgroups,<br><br>Discussion of proposed solutions,<br><br>Group feedback.<br><br>WS deliver provides additional feedback on group findings after the initial discussion.<br><br>Add personal | Charts / slides as prepared by | Workgroups<br><br>WS Deliverer |

| Time Table | Topics | Method and Goals | Material/s | Who |
|---|---|---|---|---|
| | | experience/best practice advice. | | |
| 60 minutes<br><br>*14.15-15.15* | Results of workgroups | Presentation and discussion | Group activity | Participants and WS Deliverer |
| 15 minutes<br>*15.15 – 15.30* | Mid-afternoon Break | | | |
| 60 minutes<br><br>*15.30 – 16.30* | Managers' Pre-selected Exercise<br><br><br><br><br>Goal setting | Points pre-selected by participants, based on the Project Score Card.<br><br>Participants to team up<br><br>Participants to display principles of teamwork<br><br>Participants' listing of individual goals for the next 4 weeks. | Participants to write their goals and objectives.<br><br><br>Should be copied to team member/s, as a reference.<br><br>One copy to WS deliverer/coach, listing the goals the participant would like to achieve. | Teams |

| Time Table | Topics | Method and Goals | Material/s | Who |
|---|---|---|---|---|
| | | Participants to list the top 3 things they want to achieve within the next 4 weeks. Participants to define the support they will require. Goals identified for the coaching period. | | |
| 60 minutes  16.30 – 17.30 | Goal setting discussion.  Share goals, if possible. | Participants should be encouraged to share goals.  Statement as to whether the WS assisted in achieving the goals. | Goal documentation of the participants | Participants |
| DAY THREE 15 minutes | Recap of day 2 | Presentation | Displayed via beamer with | WS Deliverer |

| Time Table | Topics | Method and Goals | Material/s | Who |
|---|---|---|---|---|
| *09:00 – 09:15* | | | reference to wall material | |
| 60 minutes<br><br>*09.15 – 10.15* | Summing up of results | WS Deliverer to sum up exercise findings.<br><br>Groups of participants to select Speaker to represent their findings. | Presentation | WS deliverer<br><br>Particpants/ group leaders |
| | Tutoring Process and future activities organising. | Presentation by group leaders to those present | | |
| | Agree on individual schedules. | Explain what happens after the WS<br><br>Naming of coach | | |

| Time Table | Topics | Method and Goals | Material/s | Who |
|---|---|---|---|---|
| | | and subsequent steps for mentoring.<br><br>Explain confidentiality of conversations between coach and participants. | | |
| 15 minutes<br>*10.15 – 10.30* | Mid-morning Break | | | |
| 60 minutes<br>*10.30 – 11.30* | Tutoring Process and future activities organising. | Explain what happens after the WS | Presentation | WS deliverer |
| 60 minutes<br><br>*11.30 – 12.30* | Agree on individual schedules. | Naming of coach and subsequent steps for mentoring. | Presentation | WS deliverer |

| Time Table | Topics | Method and Goals | Material/s | Who |
|---|---|---|---|---|
|  |  | Explain confidentiality of conversations between coach and participants. |  |  |
| 45 minutes<br>*12:30 – 13.15* | BREAK for LUNCH |  |  |  |
| 60 minutes<br><br>*13.15 – 14.15* | Assessment and Skills Evaluation<br><br>Conclusion of WS. | Ascertain that objectives have been met.<br><br>Offer additional support, if any specific topics were not fulfilled. | Discussion<br><br>Counselling | WS deliverer and participants |
| 15 minutes<br>*14.15 – 14.30* | Mid-afternoon Break |  |  |  |

| Time Table | Topics | Method and Goals | Material/s | Who |
|---|---|---|---|---|
| 30 minutes<br>*14.30 – 15.00* | Filling in of course evaluation form. | Participants' feedback and comments regarding the WS. | Round table discussion | Participants |

## 9.4 Workshop Details

| Goals: | 1. Train and intensify Project Management disciplines based on requirements of target audience. |
| --- | --- |
| | 2. Compile and review of Project Management deliverables, based on a Case Study using processes and templates. |
| | 3. Knowledge assimilation of corporation's methodological standards and their links to industry standards. |
| | 4. Facilitated exchange of participants' experiences. |
| | 5. Counselling and coaching of participants on project related and related activities through (a max 4 week) tutoring phase. |
| Prerequisites: | 1. Individual Development Plan (IDP) must be in place. |

| | |
|---|---|
| | 2. Knowledge and experience about Project Management methods. |
| | 3. Knowledge and experience about methods overview & navigation. |
| | 4. Participants should be engaged in leading project/s most of their time. |
| Content: | 1. Pre-workshop Arrangements for Participants: |
| | • Reading and understanding the Abstract of the Case Study supplied, |
| | • Comprehension of the Project Management (PM) Key Areas, their modules and narrative, |
| | • Filling in of the PM Key Areas self-assessment form, |
| | • Understanding the Case Study Score Card and its components, |
| | • Reading the Workshop Agenda and drafting additional needs, if necessary. |
| | 2. Subjects included in the Workshop: |
| | • Discussion based on the Pre-workshop activities, |

- Benefits of Project Management,

- Project Management functions and the interfacing of the company's and Industry standards,

- Functional skills for Programme/Project Managers,

- The impact of Project Management within the organisation,

- Processes, templates usage and PM best practices,

- Group exercise based on Case Study,

- Discussion on Post-workshop coaching.

3. Focus on Project Management disciplines (workshop modules) according to the Case Study work:

For every workshop module there will be:

- Brief discussion of theory.

| | |
|---|---|
| | • Practical (case study based) exercises in groups.<br><br>• Facilitated discussion of deliverables and exchange of experience<br><br>4. Organising the coaching phase, which follows the workshop:<br><br>• Define the participant's individual goals.<br><br>• Agree individual development activities for the four weeks of coaching. |
| Methods: | 1. Pre-workshop:<br><br>Abstract of Case Study, PM Key Areas self-assessment form, Case Study Score Card and workshop agenda.<br><br>2. Interactive workshop:<br><br>Consisting of different interfacing modules and based on a generic Case Study with integrated exercises, followed by tutoring. PM Key Areas self-assessment form for workshop, Score Card for Case Study assessment. |

| | |
|---|---|
| | 3. Post-workshop:<br><br>PM Key Areas self-assessment form, coaching agreement for main points raised and overall schedule for mentoring. |
| Duration: | Three days workshop, followed by four weeks of tutoring phase. |
| Developed by: | Department responsible for Service Excellence |
| Costs: | Local Workshop Deliverer and participant's effort and expenses. |

# 10. SUCCESSFUL IMPLEMENTATION

## 10.1 Non-acceptance

One of the greatest threats in Projects Management is the non-acceptance of it or misuse of the system by the organisation's own personnel. Obtaining their buy-in is essential. It is obvious that someone is going to be appointed to ensure that the change management principles are adhered to and the system maintained throughout the organisation.

It is, also, important that if information leaves the organisation by its transference to others for use on the company's behalf, that they have adequate systems to protect the set standards.

The successful implementation of Project Management is reliant upon people and in particular the employees whose contracts of employment may need adjustment to protect the company and the adequate management and execution of plans for the solution to the threats caused by the changes identified.

## 10.2 Programme Management

Programme Management may have many responsibilities, but the most important of all is the ability to identify and positively execute plans to manage the changes threatening the objectives.

Through a process of structured interviews and plans the Assessment Analysis is used to highlight the specific requests for changes, which may turn into risks. During the interviews Assessment Analysis is used to capture the key changes from the interviewees.

In turn, the Assessment Analysis provides a life-cycle process, which highlights the primary prioritisation of the changes. In large, complex, and critical programmes, it is essential that a true prioritised report is available so that the imminent changes can be managed first.

The process commences by identifying the most important changes, which may become threats to a project. These are given priority, support and management expertise. Once the prioritisation exercise is completed, the participating people are notified and subsequently interviewed to bring out and capture any possible changes they may have.

Within a programme, projects are prioritised to ensure that those most critical to the programme's success are given priority to scarce resources.

## 10.3 METHODOLOGY

The Management of Change allows the capture of collective knowledge and expertise from those involved on the project, in a form that facilitates the communication of changes, their assessments, and the pro-active management of the changes requested.

In essence, this is the mechanism by which the functions of Information Technology programmes and projects are held together as a result of the principles operating within the methodology for the management of change, as in the S:I:G:M:A: paragraphs below:

- Systematic: The varied Changes, their Assessments, and the consequential Risks relating to or consisting of a system.

Methodical in procedures and plans, these are addressed to those involved and deliberating within the parameters of their systems development responsibilities.

- Integration: The results being dependable on the mutual or reciprocal action which encourages those involved in the programs and projects to communicate with each other and to work closely with a view to solving the threatening changes before they impact on the development of the system.

- Generic: The individuals involved maintain an approach, which relates and characterises the whole group of those involved in assessing the changes and attacking any threatening ones before they become risks to the development of the system. The end result being the avoidance of apparent problems within the pre-defined users' systems requirements.

- Methodology: Following the system architects and the change management practitioners enable this. Simply follow the approved body of systems development methods, rules and management procedures employed by their organisation. For practical or even ethical reasons, it must be noted that with such a philosophy, it is seldom possible to fulfil all requirements of very large organisational systems.

- Applications: As such, Change Management is administered by putting to use such techniques and in applying the Change Management

principles in the development of various applications will involve numerous and varied activities.

A concrete issue in developing new applications is the problem of communication among the people involved, the motivation constantly needed for generic work, the ability to interact systematically and in using Change Management.

## 11. PROJECTS MANAGEMENT WORKSHOP SLIDES

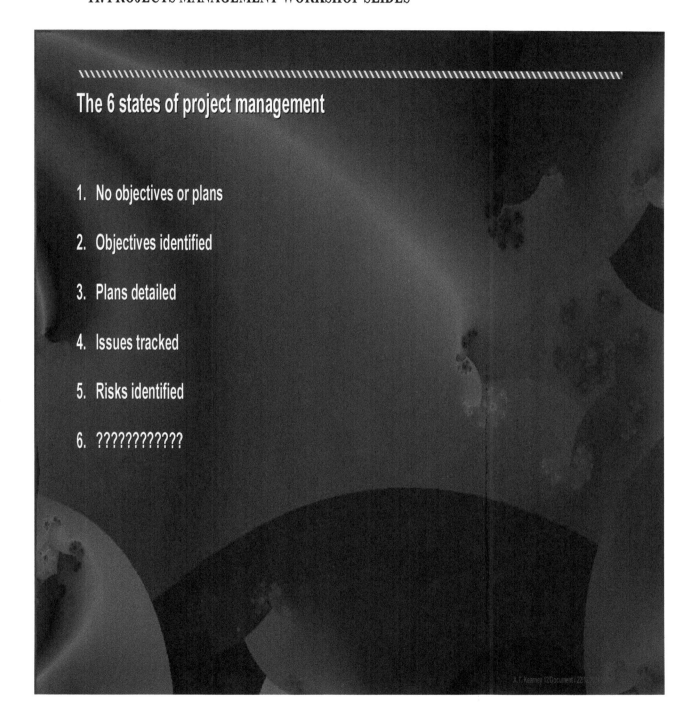

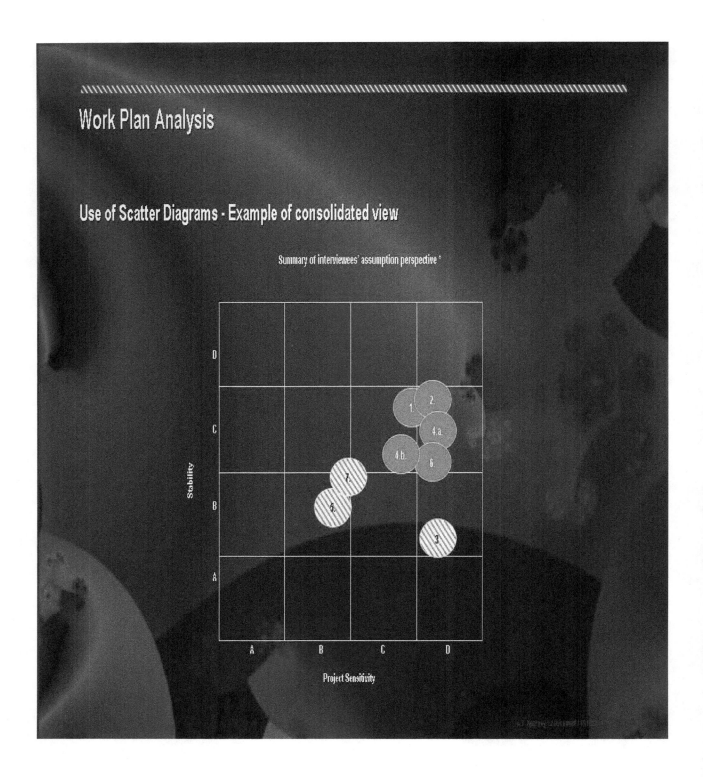

*Andreas Sofroniou*

## Work Plan Analysis

### Use of Scatter Diagrams - Example of views on one assumption

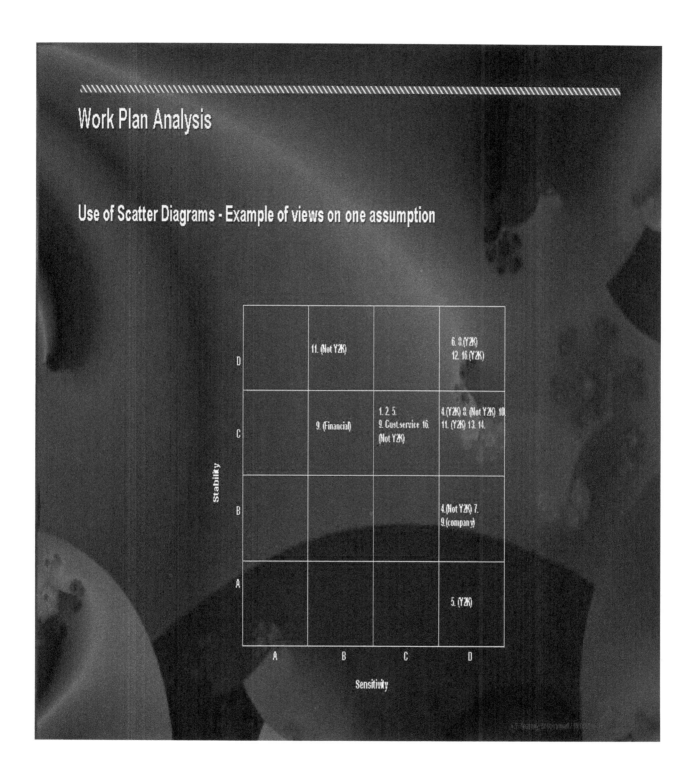

*Andreas Sofroniou*

# Work Plan Analysis

## Use of Scatter Diagrams

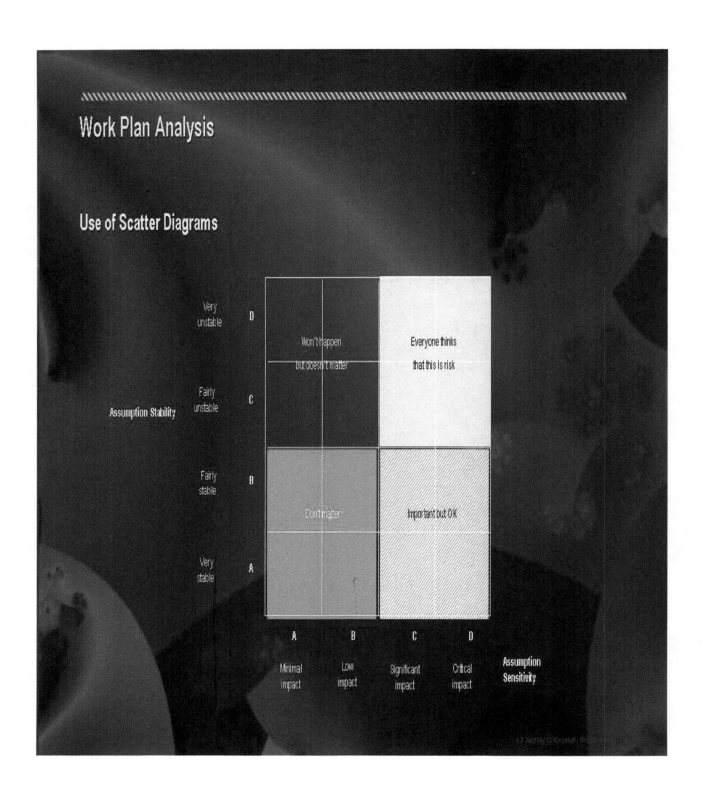

# Work Plan Analysis

## Pre-selected assumptions - Example

- 1. Create the case for change
  - All critical benefits identified in the business case will prove realistic and be achieved

- 2. Manage the programme
  - The current governance structure, processes and plans will prove adequate to successfully deliver the programme

- 3. Align, engage and mobilise leadership
  - Senior management and project sponsors will continue to be committed to, engaged with all key aspects of the programme

- 4. Align, engage and mobilise organisation .......

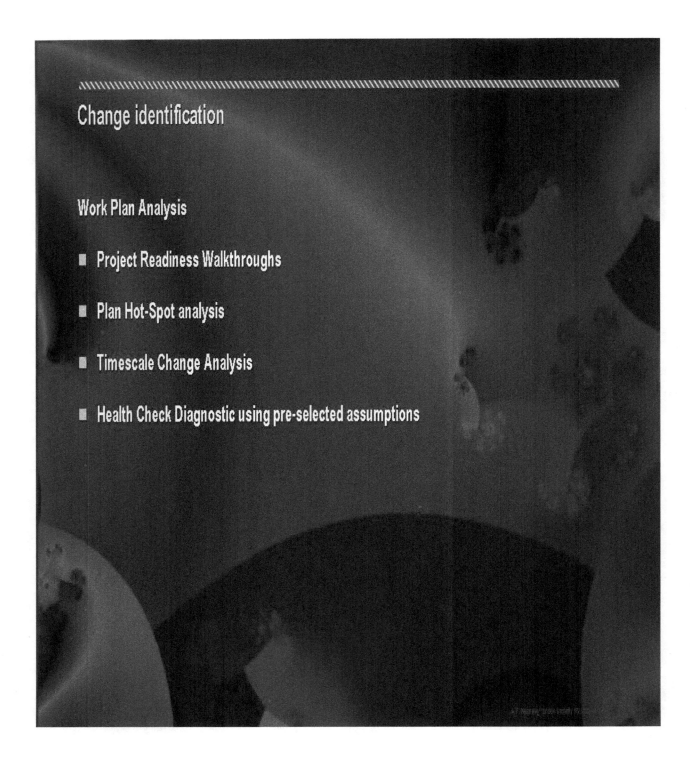

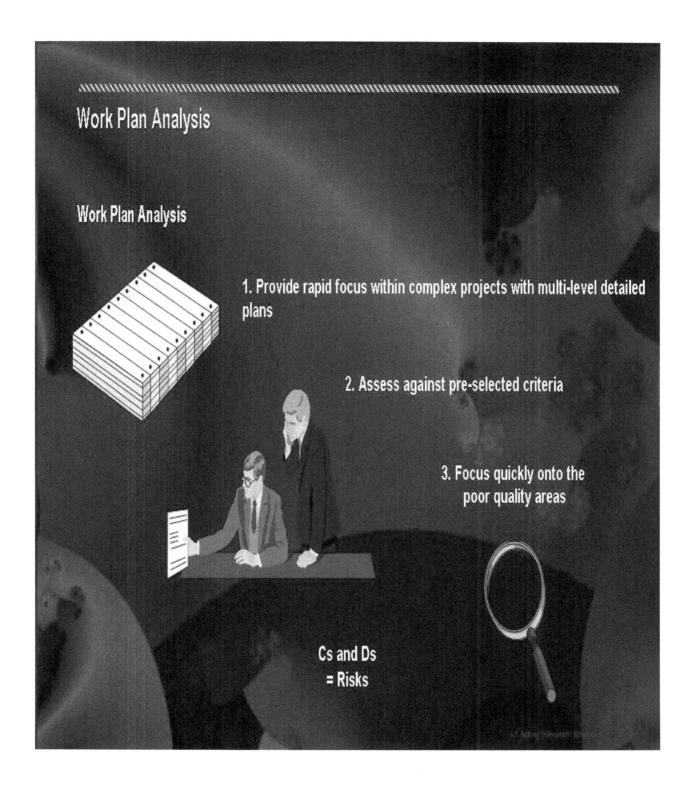

Work Plan Analysis

Work Plan Analysis

1. Provide rapid focus within complex projects with multi-level detailed plans

2. Assess against pre-selected criteria

3. Focus quickly onto the poor quality areas

Cs and Ds
= Risks

*Andreas Sofroniou*

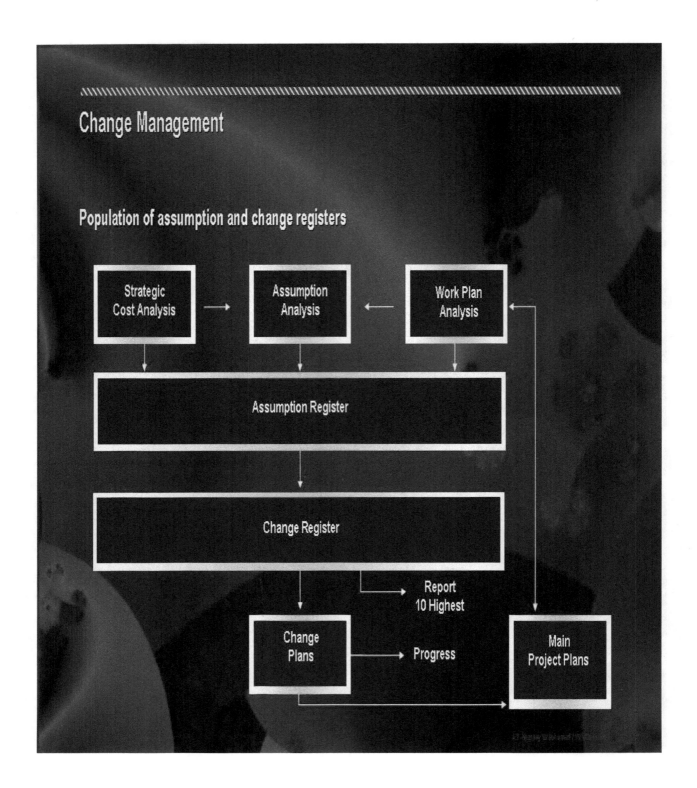

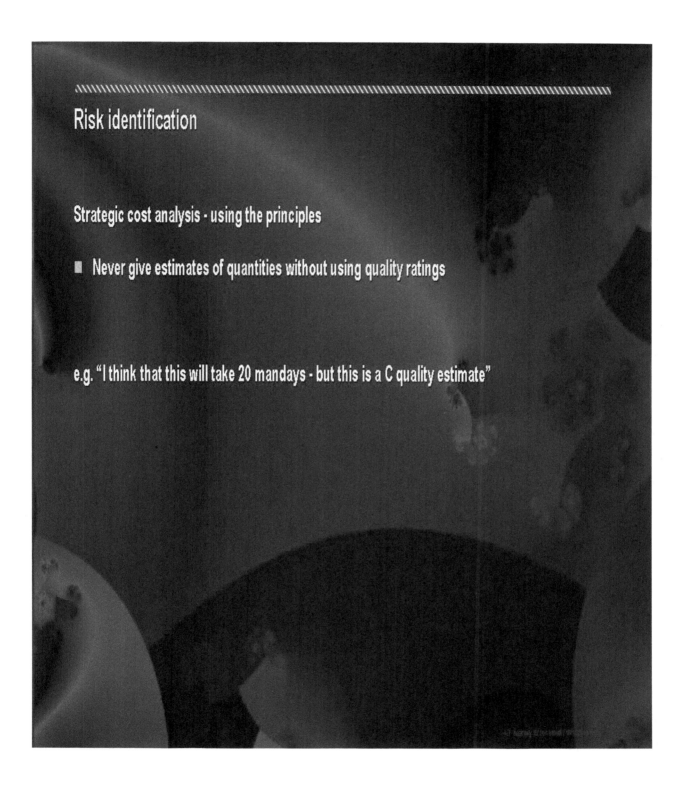

# Risk identification

Strategic cost analysis - using the principles

- Never give estimates of quantities without using quality ratings

e.g. "I think that this will take 20 mandays - but this is a C quality estimate"

# Change identification

Strategic cost analysis

- Refines normal approaches to cost estimating

- Helps to quantify total cost uncertainty in a project

- Encourages objective contingency budget setting

- Can be used in difficult price negotiations

- Allows a risk budget approach

- Kick-starts the risk assessment process

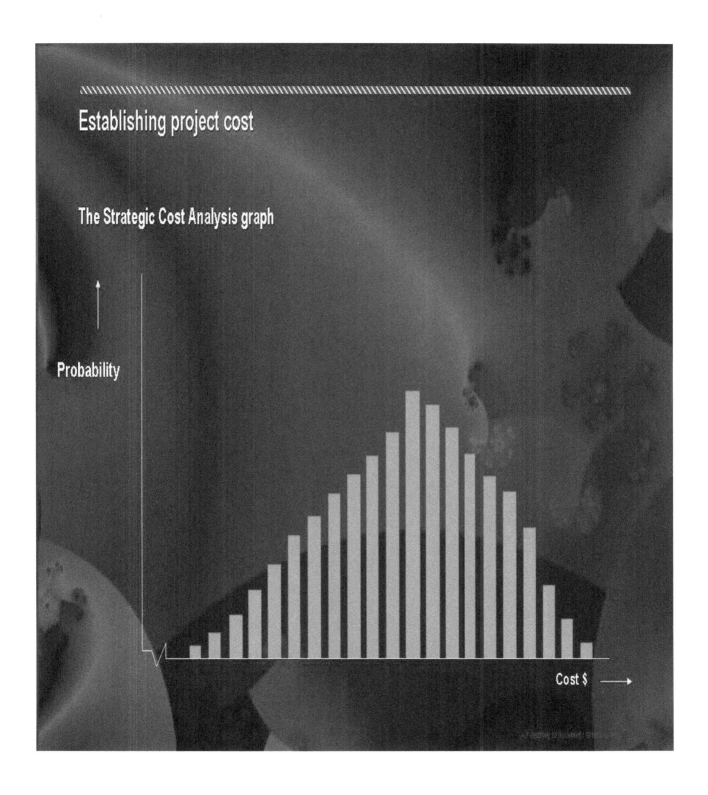

*Andreas Sofroniou*

# Change identification — Strategic Cost Analysis

## The quality of the estimate

- The notion of 'bricks' allows us to investigate the quality of the estimate

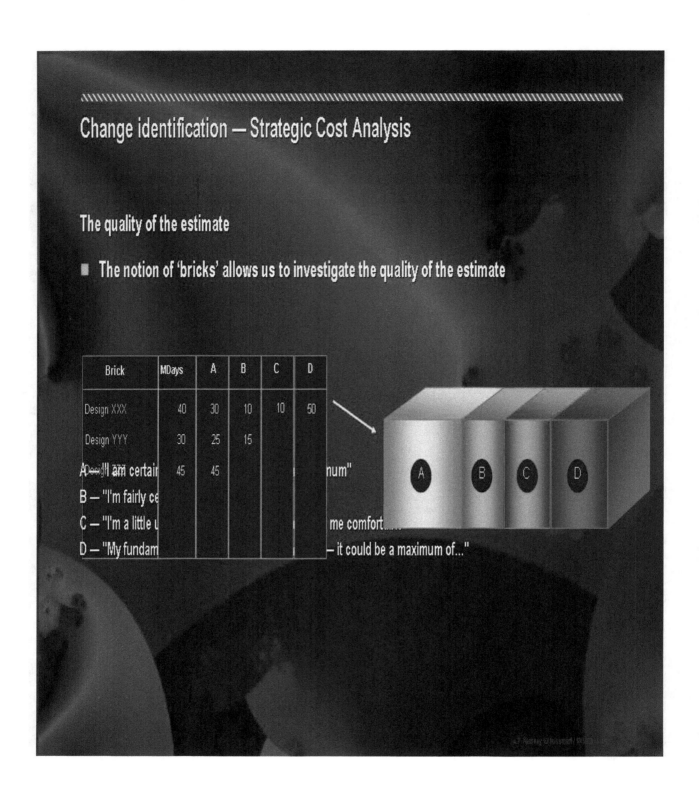

| Brick | MDays | A | B | C | D |
|-------|-------|-----|-----|-----|-----|
| Design XXX | 40 | 30 | 10 | 10 | 50 |
| Design YYY | 30 | 25 | 15 | | |
| Design ZZZ | 45 | 45 | | | |

A — "I am certain ... num"

B — "I'm fairly ce

C — "I'm a little u me comfort.....

D — "My fundam – it could be a maximum of..."

## Change identification — Strategic Cost Analysis

**The project Brick Wall contains all project cost elements**

- Vertical Bricks are one offs — they occur at a certain point in the project (e.g. to implement a piece of software is a Vertical Brick)

- Horizontal Bricks continue throughout the project (e.g. Project Management is a Horizontal Brick)

- Total project cost is signified by a complete "Brick Wall"

*Andreas Sofroniou*

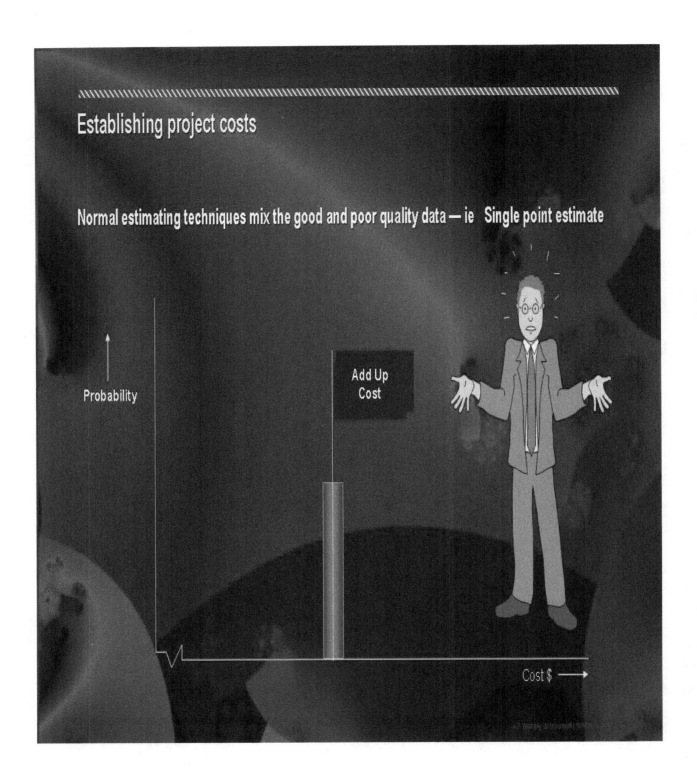

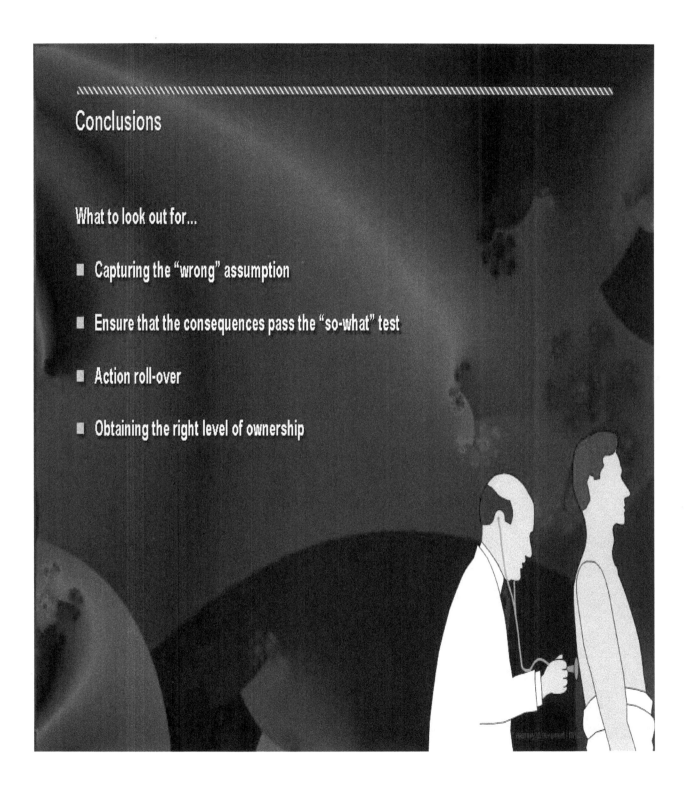

## Conclusions

What to look out for...

- Capturing the "wrong" assumption

- Ensure that the consequences pass the "so-what" test

- Action roll-over

- Obtaining the right level of ownership

*Andreas Sofroniou*

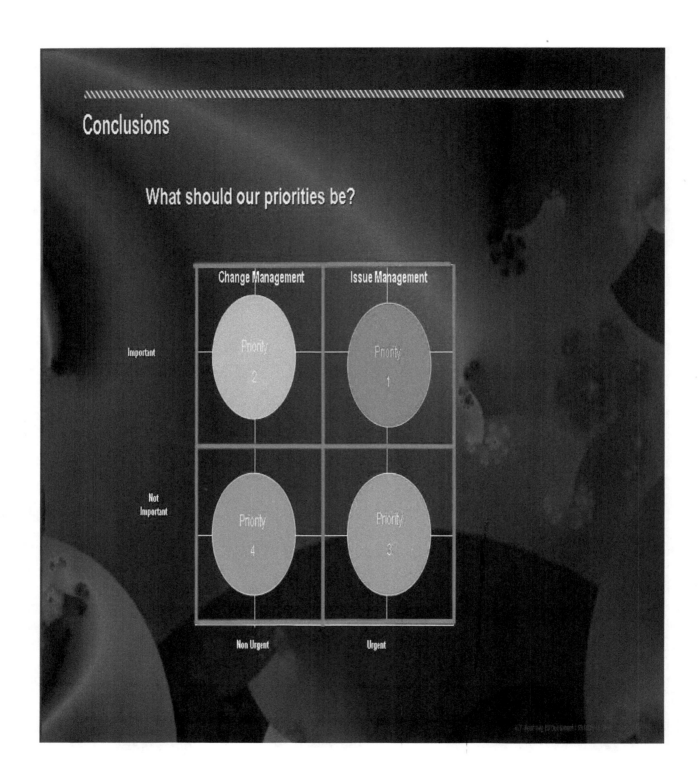

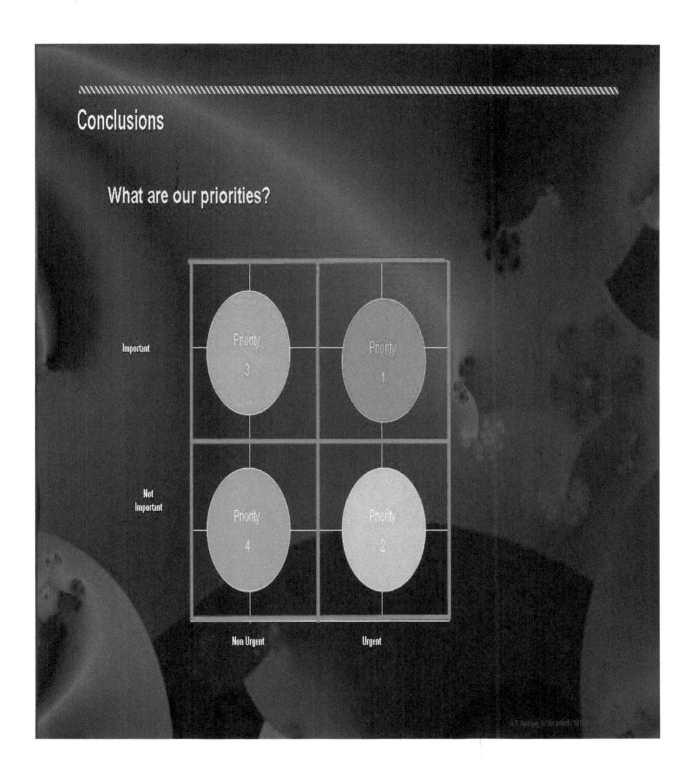

*Andreas Sofroniou*

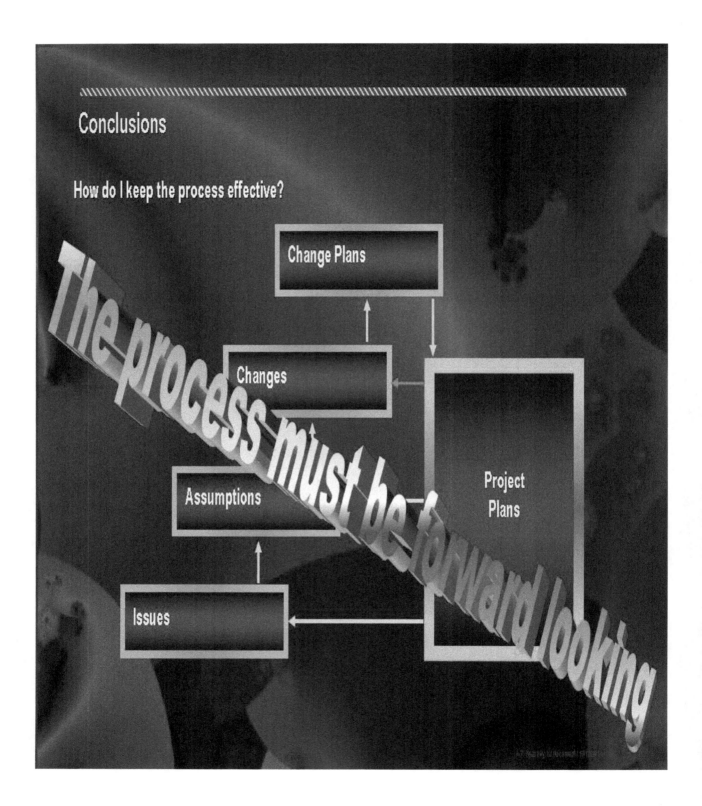

*Andreas Sofroniou*

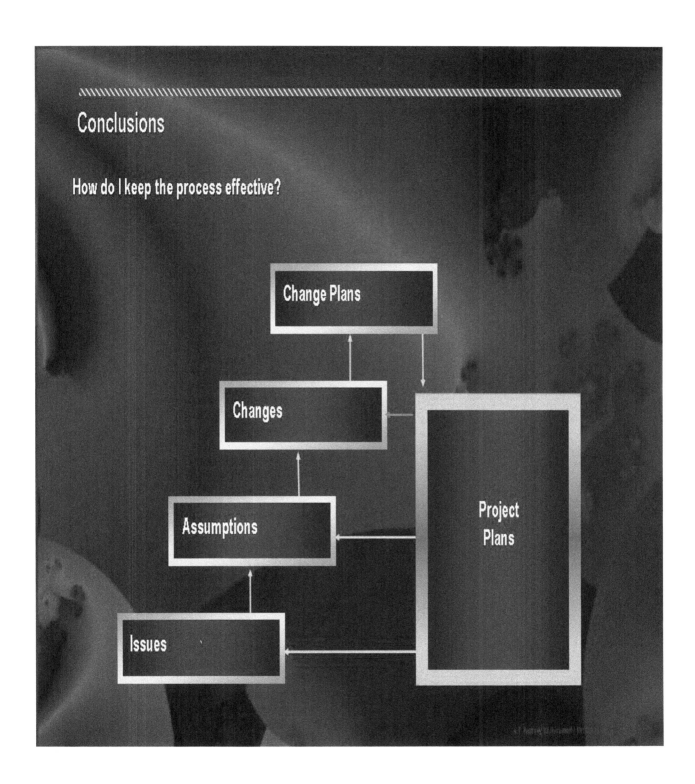

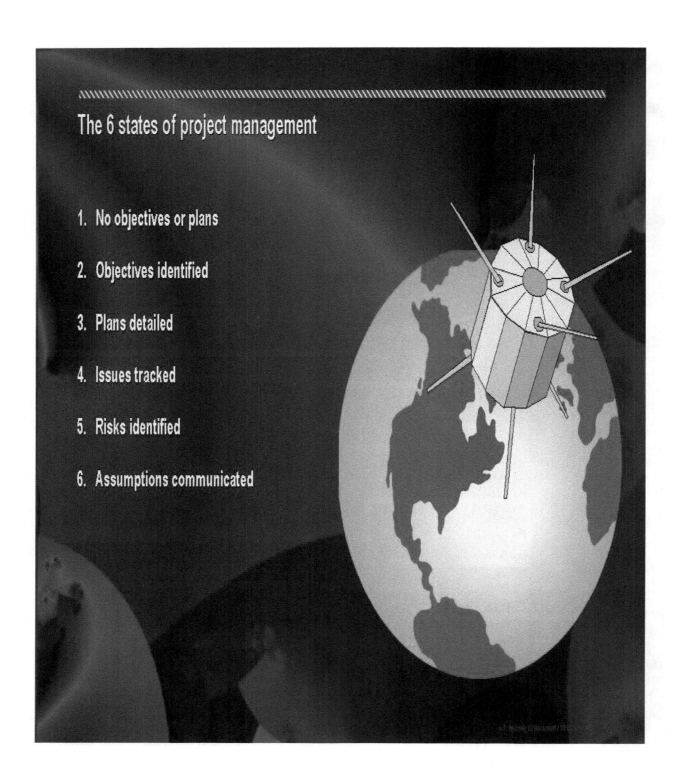

The 6 states of project management

1. No objectives or plans

2. Objectives identified

3. Plans detailed

4. Issues tracked

5. Risks identified

6. Assumptions communicated

# Conclusions

Who in the organisation will see the benefits of Change Management In I.T. clearly?

- Head of the organization = CEO?

- One step down = CFO/CIO?

- Programme Director

- Project Manager

Depends on the role and management style of the management team
    Hands on - hard sell
    Hands off - easy sell

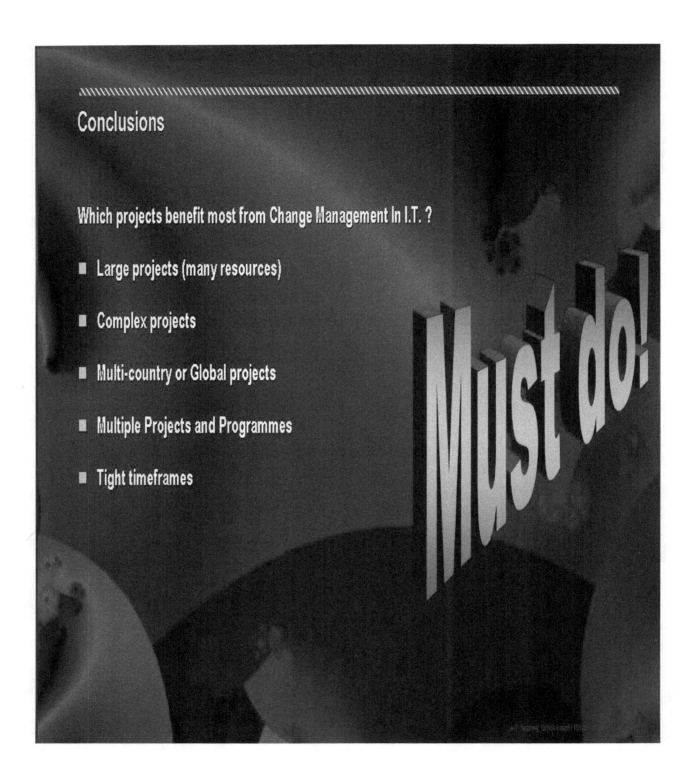

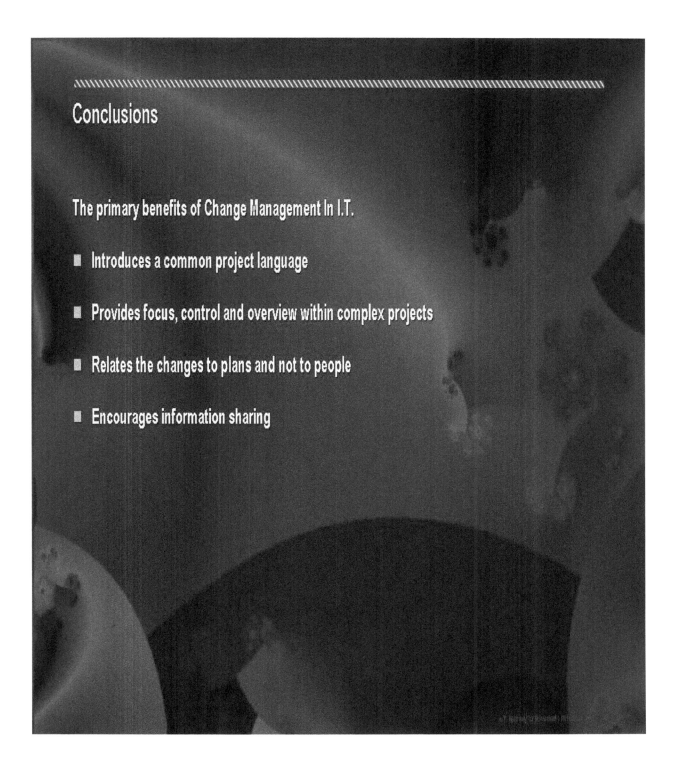

## Conclusions

The primary benefits of Change Management In I.T.

- Introduces a common project language

- Provides focus, control and overview within complex projects

- Relates the changes to plans and not to people

- Encourages information sharing

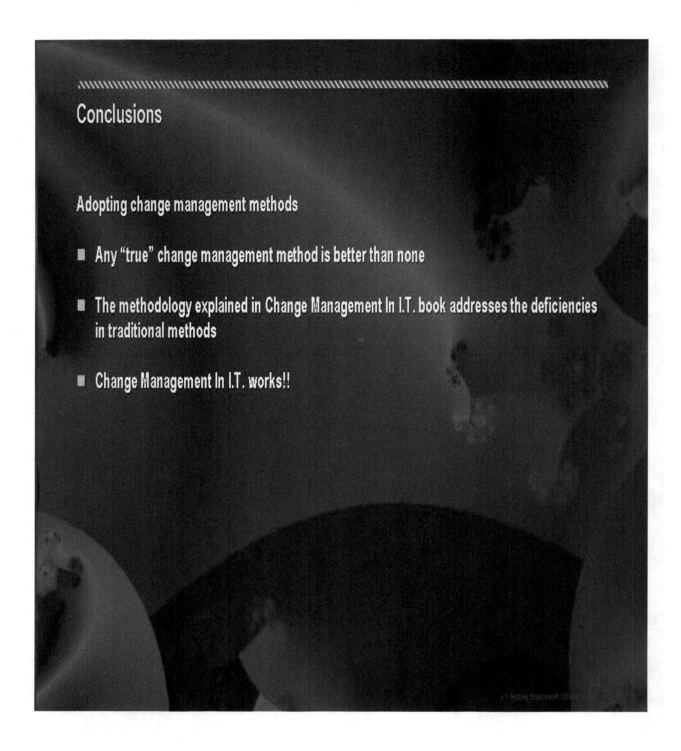

## Conclusions

Adopting change management methods

- Any "true" change management method is better than none

- The methodology explained in Change Management In I.T. book addresses the deficiencies in traditional methods

- Change Management In I.T. works!!

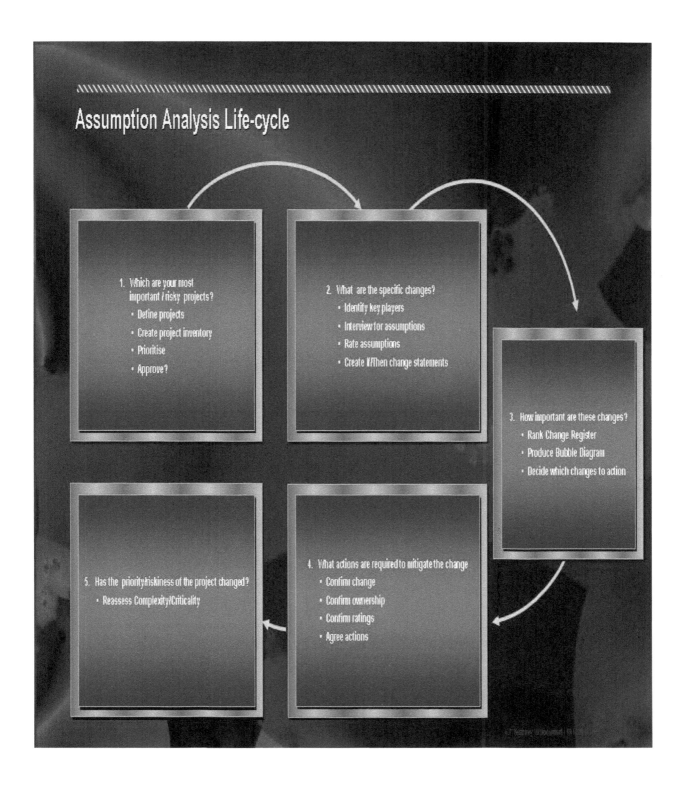

*Andreas Sofroniou*

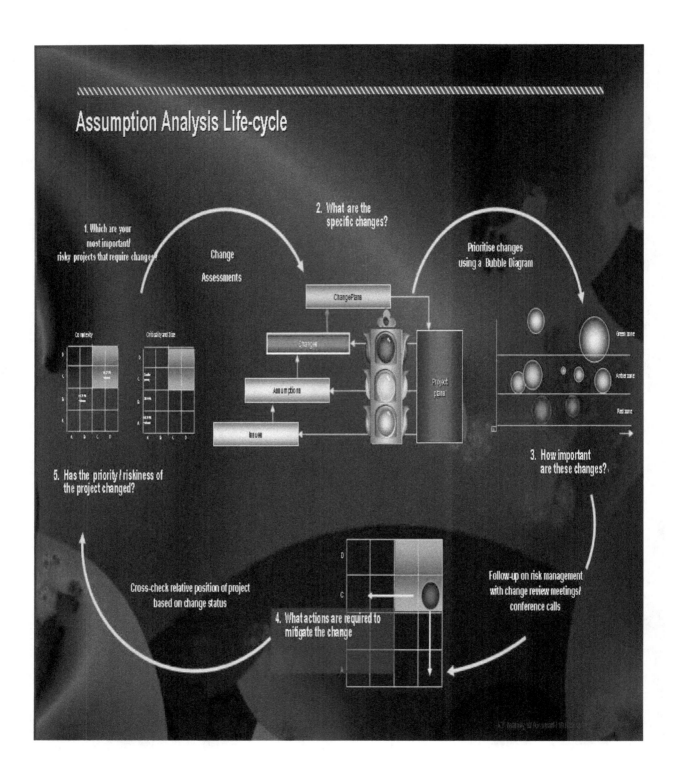

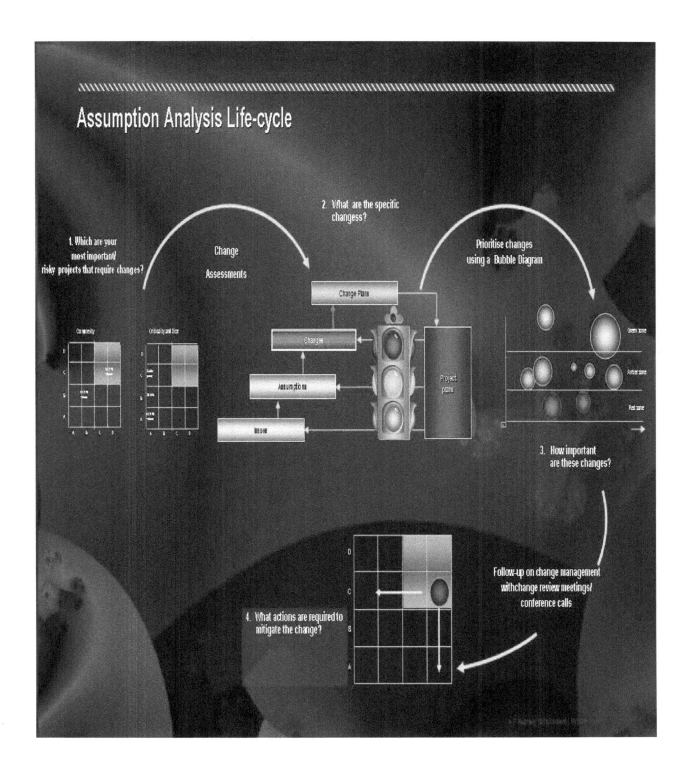

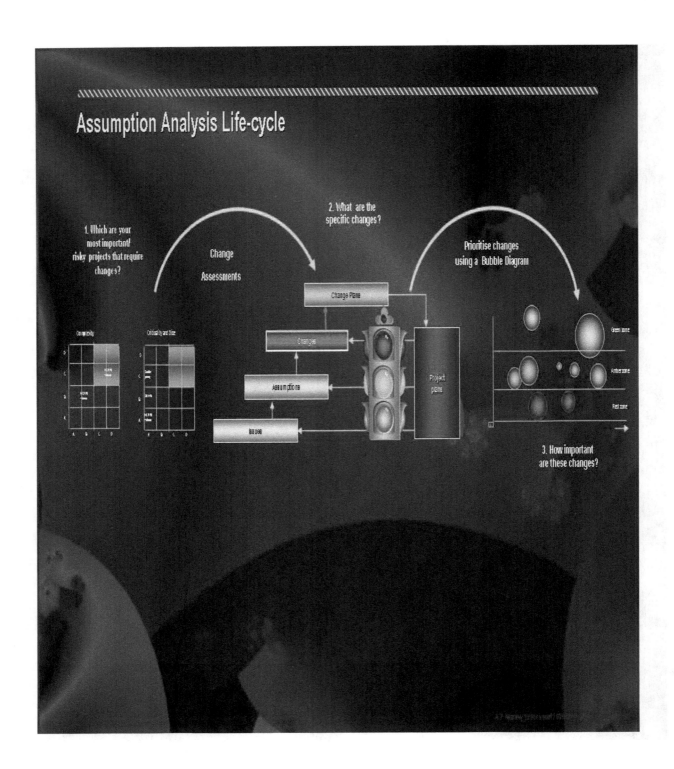

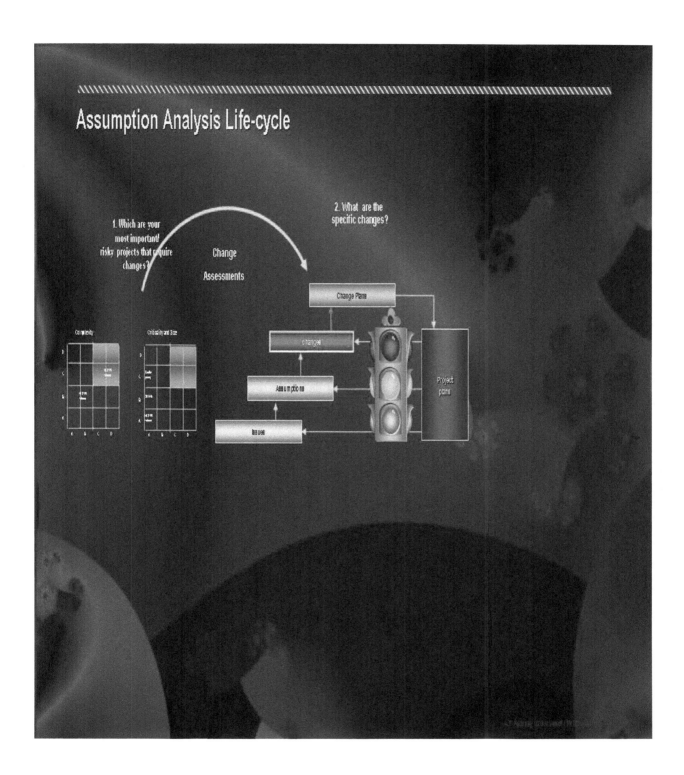

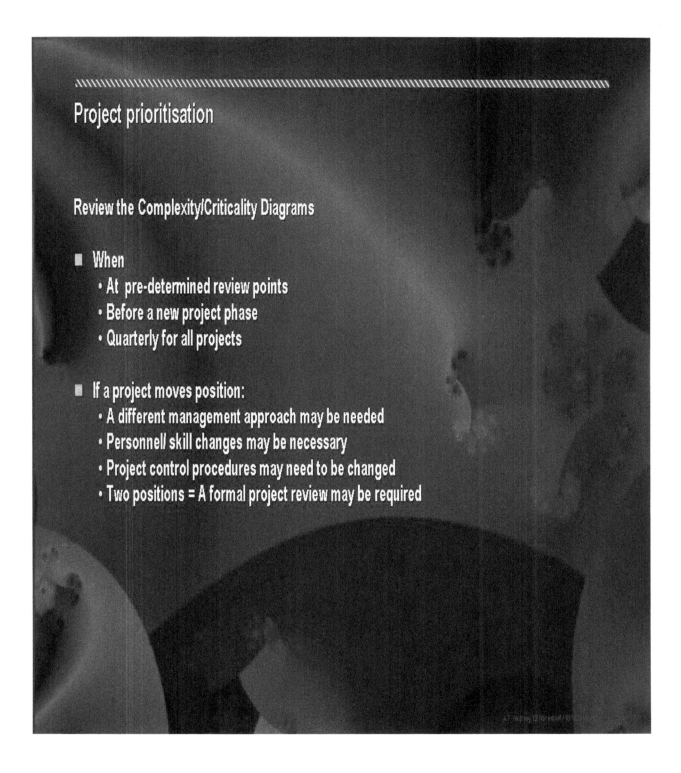

## Project prioritisation

Review the Complexity/Criticality Diagrams

- **When**
  - At pre-determined review points
  - Before a new project phase
  - Quarterly for all projects

- **If a project moves position:**
  - A different management approach may be needed
  - Personnel/ skill changes may be necessary
  - Project control procedures may need to be changed
  - Two positions = A formal project review may be required

*Andreas Sofroniou*

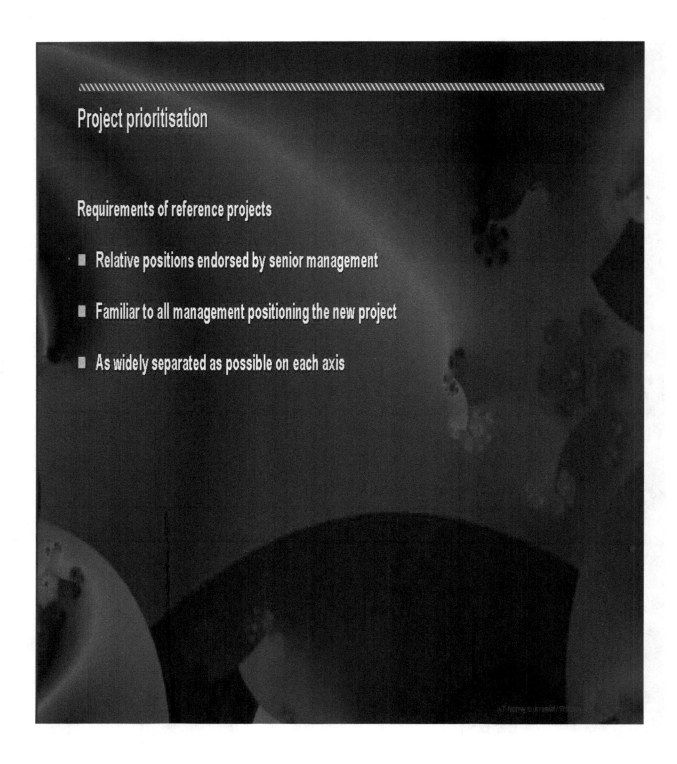

**Project prioritisation**

Requirements of reference projects

■ Relative positions endorsed by senior management

■ Familiar to all management positioning the new project

■ As widely separated as possible on each axis

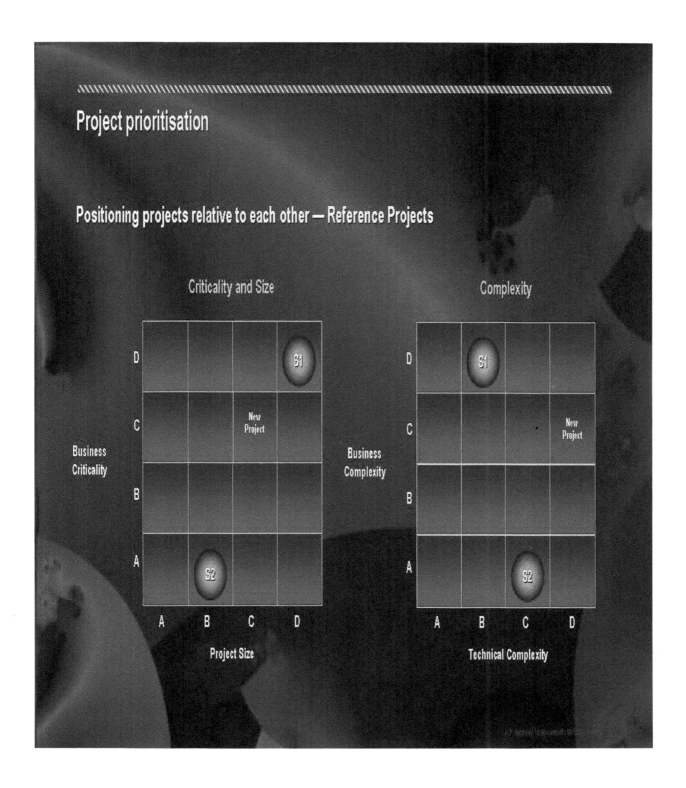

*Andreas Sofroniou*

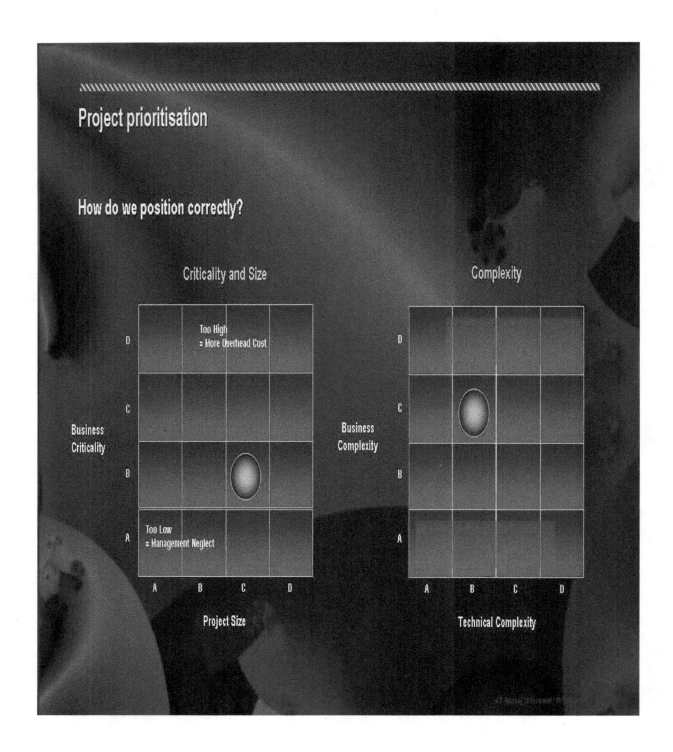

*Andreas Sofroniou*

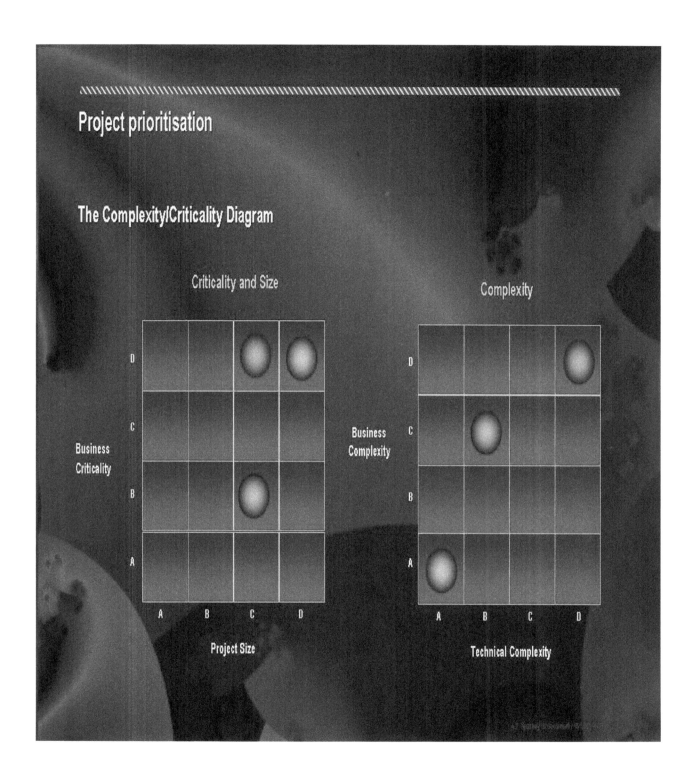

# Project prioritisation

## The Complexity/Criticality Diagram

*Andreas Sofroniou*

# Project prioritisation

## Prioritisation using Complexity and Criticality

- Business Criticality — How much does it matter if the project fails to meet its objectives (CSFs)  A = nice to have, D = Critical to business

- Project Size — How much will the project (development and implementation) cost?  A = smallest team, D = largest team

- Business Complexity — How many areas of the business will be involved in the project?  A = one area, D = all/many areas

- Technical Complexity — How technically difficult is the project?
  A = simple/familiar technology/solution, D = new technology/scale never attempted etc

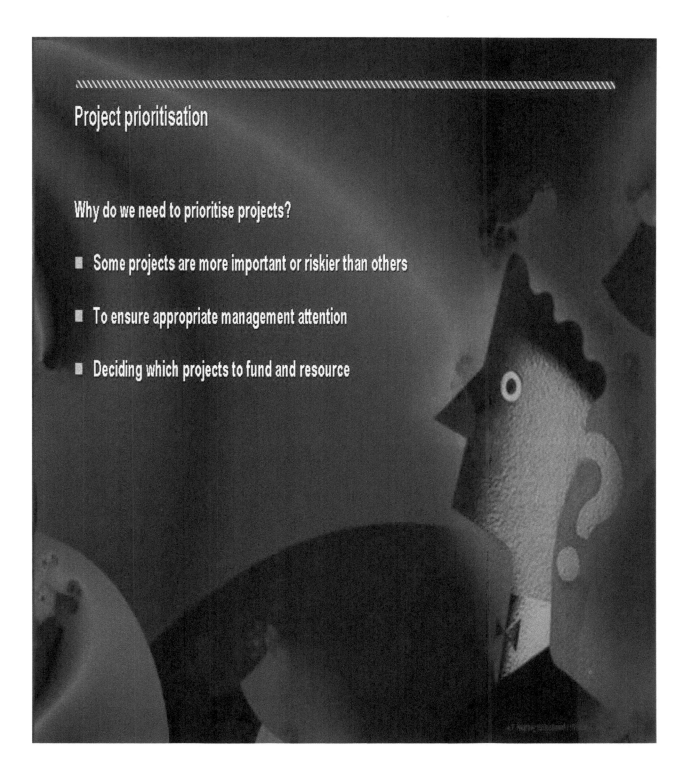

## Project prioritisation

Why do we need to prioritise projects?

- Some projects are more important or riskier than others

- To ensure appropriate management attention

- Deciding which projects to fund and resource

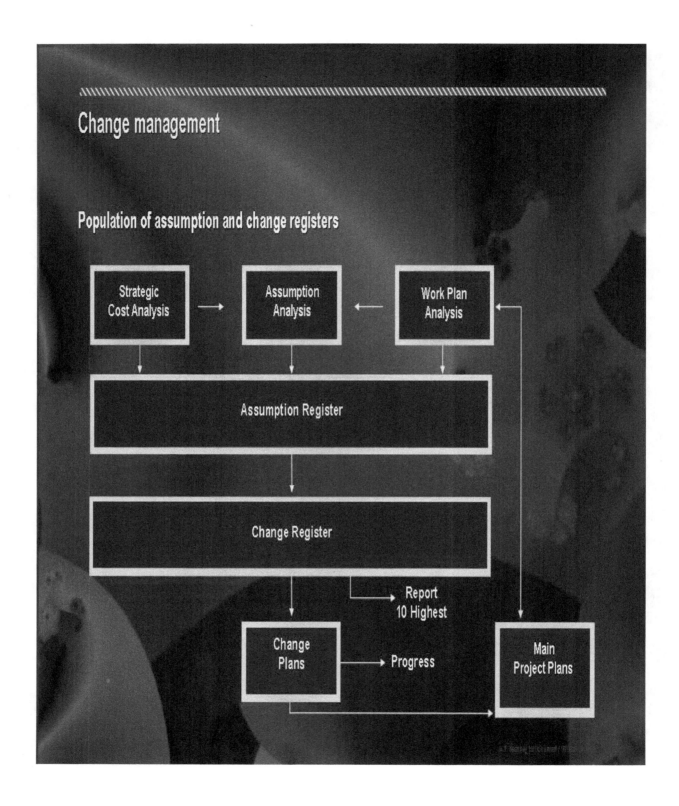

# Change identification

**Work Plan Analysis - the principles**

- Used as a "quick and dirty" tool

- Agree criteria for assessment with project "sponsor"

- Get the team's view, not your view

- Feed back the consensus view

## 12. A COLLABORATIVE APPROACH TO MANAGING A *TIME CRITICAL PROJECT*

### 12.1 Abstract

The implementation of a time critical project requires a large number of soft skills in addition to the standard set of project management hard skills and supporting toolsets to ensure successful delivery on time and within budget. This paper will provide an example of a case study of how a successful collaboration was achieved between two fictional organisations in the U.K.

The following topics of interest to project managers will be covered in this paper:

1. Establishment of ground rules for the engagement and the 'modus operandi'

2. Determination of requirements process - soft skills required

3. Team empowerment and skill sets and how this fits into a structured project management environment

4. How the project managers of each organisation adopted an empowering and collaborative management style

5. Internal and external issues that had to be overcome in adopting this collaborative approach

6. How the project managers knew if they had been successful in meeting the objectives of both organizations - the mechanisms that existed for formal and informal reviews

## 12.2 Background and Establishment of Ground Rules

Legislative Background and Consultation Processes

How the work was commissioned.

- A consultation exercise invited views on the format of a replacement scheme.

- The identifier protects the interests of the retail trade.

- Following this consultation, managers decided that from September 2015, the new system would include a new set of requirements.

The following table represents the key milestones of the project agreed in order to meet the deadlines:

| | |
|---|---|
| Requirements gathering | May - July |
| Project start up commences | July |
| Business Requirements | July |
| New Development (phased) | September - August |
| Approved | April |

## 12.3 Summary of Soft Skills displayed in the Project

The project involved changes of approximately 4500 function points. This was a mixture of new development and changes to existing functionality, all of which had to be thoroughly tested involving most of the partners listed above.

The program of work was set up using structured methodologies. The key message from this project is that to make a collaboration work, a number of key soft skills and behavioural styles must be present in addition to the standard hard skills of planning, scheduling, monitoring, and controlling.

The following is a summary of those skills with a number of practical examples:

Right People with Ability to Communicate and Resolve Conflict

The right people had to be in place and had to be able to specify requirements that could be understood by the system designers and then translated into executable code. It was important for staff working on the project to have communications skills as well as technical skills.

*[Soft skill – communication lines had to be open between all relevant parties and many questions asked to seek clarifications. The resolution of conflict was key in the requirements gathering phase.]*

Establish Trust

Trust had to be established

*[Soft skill – the project managers had to be able to trust each other and be able to communicate good and bad news in an environment of 'no blame'. The focus was on speedy resolution of issues taking whatever steps were needed.]*

12.4 Establishing the right climate for collaboration

The project managers in setting up the framework for the project established a mechanism to have a single integrated high-level project plan with shared success criteria, a single integrated team spanning the two organizations.

*[Soft skill – the project managers had to use negotiation and persuasion to convince management on both sides that the successful outcome was more important than a rigid process-driven ideology. Both PRINCE and the proprietary project management methodology allow tailoring which resulted in the flexibility needed]*

Pro-activity when dealing with external communications

Pro-activity had to be displayed when dealing with the many customers who were involved in the project as testers of changed functionality and also when dealing with the media

*[Soft skill – the project managers had to adopt different roles during the life of the project. These roles frequently required the ability to 'think outside the box' and to be creative in thinking to overcome obstacles.]*

## 12.5 Culture Change

Culture changes had to be made. The relationship is governed by a traditional contract between a customer and a supplier for IT services. Both organisations were keen to move to a culture where partnership was the mechanism for achieving change.

This project was one of the pioneers of this way of working

[*Soft skill – coaching and mentoring of all staff had to take place to examine and change some of the traditional behaviours that existed in both. This involved appreciation of the different styles of negotiating and the move to a less confrontational way of working. The achievement of win-win for all parties was seen as desirable but achieved in a democratic manner, with some humour displayed in the process.*]

The following sections will illustrate how some of the attitudes and soft skills summarized above were used during the life cycle of the project at different phases and activities.

## 12.6 Process for Requirements Determination

The starting point for the delivery of the technical part of the project involved the establishment of a detailed requirement and the process and soft skills involved are described below.

The soft skills involved in this process are only used as an illustration.

In the case of this time-critical project delivery, it was important to establish from the outset that we were all 'in the right jungle' as it was seen by both parties in the shared risk analysis that the project could not afford to have an incomplete or ambiguous scope.

Both collaborators worked jointly to establish an approach to gathering the requirements using Joint Application Design (JAD) techniques. Workshops were arranged and jointly facilitated by the staff involved. The participants or stakeholders in the JAD sessions were all those people who had an interest in any aspect of the change of UK format and those experienced designers/developers who needed to understand the requirements specified. Both project managers attended the JAD sessions.

It was agreed from the outset that a collaborative style of working would best ensure a win-win outcome. The goals of both had to be taken into account in discussions and alignment of these would result in a successful win-win outcome.

An open and honest style of project management was adopted from the outset with regular informal discussions being just as important as the more formal meetings that were put in place as part of the mechanism to run the project in accordance with the Prince 2 methodology.

The key soft skill that was important in the facilitated workshops and contributed to a successful outcome was the active management of conflict. Conflict results in an unclear or ambiguous requirement and it was important with the tight timescales that the requirement was not only detailed but was unambiguous and was seen as feasible to implement.

## 12.7 Other key soft skills and behavioural traits

- To be able to ask the searching question even if it might appear to be *'dumb'*.

- To be able to negotiate for a win-win outcome (it was important to see the points of view from all sides)

- To be able to obtain the strong support of the project sponsor

- The consulting project manager had been trained in facilitation techniques and had successfully applied JAD techniques for other clients. The facilitator has to ensure that there is no ambiguity in the outcome.

- The company project manager had the authority to make decisions based on the sound advice given by experienced colleagues and had to have the strength to escalate internally to ensure that all relevant business areas were represented.

- The company stakeholders were empowered to make decisions on behalf of their business area and had the business knowledge to do so.

- The consultancy stakeholders were experienced designers with relevant business knowledge and who had the ability to ask searching questions.

- The ability and willingness of all the stakeholders to have a debate but then to accept that the outcome is a jointly agreed outcome for the whole team.

- Outputs from the Facilitated Workshops

12.7 The following were the outputs of the facilitated workshops:

- A draft detailed requirements document. All parties reviewed the detailed requirements document several times before a final version was agreed. This kept changes to requirement throughout the project to a minimum.

- A request by the company for a fixed-price quotation based on the detailed requirement.

- Identification and quantification of project risks and issues. These were quantified by both parties in joint review sessions and included in the fixed price quotation. A partnership approach was adopted right from the start

12.8 Team Empowerment

A synchronised organisation is like a champion rowing team - people working together with a certain rhythm that allows the group to do things the individuals could not do. Synchronisation expands the capacity of the whole group.

In other words, how team empowerment fits into a structured project management environment. An empowered team is an efficient working unit that is able to work together and make decisions.

The project managers had to display a number of soft skills and attributes to manage the projects in this collaborative way with empowered teams:

- Progress was monitored in regular checkpoint meetings. Issues, risks, and project size were also tracked via these meetings. Informal meetings were held as needed.

- The project managers adopted a leadership style that encouraged people to try and work on their own initiative but not be afraid to ask questions of anyone else in the team regardless of what part of the two organizations they sat in. Roles were clearly identified and responsibilities clearly defined.

- Set clear and measurable objectives for everyone in the team based on the understanding of the detailed requirements document. The project managers were looking for end results based on optimization of individual skill sets but playing as a team.

- Ensure that all ideas and information are considered. If a project manager has made a previously incorrect decision or a decision based on an incomplete assessment of all the relevant facts, they had to act decisively to take corrective action. Sometimes a project manager can be wrong!

- Active listening - use of play-back techniques to ensure a correct understanding of what had been said in a particular dialogue

- Senior management was by exception only as characterized in PRINCE 2.

## 12.9 Communication Strategy

A communication plan was produced which detailed all communications between the company and its external customers and with the consultants at different levels.

The formal governance structure of the project was that of PRINCE 2:

The client's project board was the vehicle for making all the major decisions on the project strategy as mandated by PRINCE 2. The consultancy project manager was a member of this board. The Steering Group oversaw the project but only became involved in major exceptions as reported by the Project Board Chairman.

## 12.10 Project Management Style

A collaborative approach to this project was adopted from the outset. It was essential to have all the staff working effectively as 'one team' from the outset. The project management style was one of openness and honesty.

The aim was to create a working environment where issues and problems were detected at the earliest possible opportunity. This meant all staff from whichever organisation working together and participating in activities that traditionally they may not have been involved with in a customer-IT supplier relationship.

The open approach and partnering approach is illustrated by the following:

- Section of both organisations were used to obtain the right project staff,

- Independent risk manager displayed listening qualities and as a result more openness in discussing and managing risk was evident,

- Sharing of estimates for work to be performed,

- Sharing of metrics information at the end of the project,

- Sharing of relevant business information during the life of the project,

   Issues to overcome in adopting a collaborative approach,

   Internal issues,

- Both teams have methodologies and procedures. These have to be synchronized with each other to ensure consistency,

- Both companies have particular organizational cultures. Both organizations needed to display a willingness to adapt. Some examples from this case study include the format and style of certain meetings, involving staff in activities that were traditionally the domain of the IT supplier (e.g. system testing),

- Both had to work within existing matrix management structures but could not let decision-making be delayed because of these structures,

99

- Conflicts of business priorities had to be handled by the Programme Director/Manager to ensure that the key work was not impacted,

- The Programme Director/Manager had to make sure that all relevant groups were involved in the planning phases and not at the last minute.

## 12.11 How project success was quantified for both organisations

The criteria for a successful project delivery were established in the Project Initiation document. Both, the consultancy and the company, shared the risks and reward of this project in the manner of partners. Neither partner would be successful on their own as the project was so high profile that any failure of one party would have been highly visible.

Informal reviews:

- Conversations between team members, work coordinators and the project managers to check and clarify understanding of requirements, design and test results,

- Telephone conversations between project managers to deal with issues, questions with the aim of communicating information as quickly as possible,

- Project managers using informal conversations in the office to pick up information, if relevant to project activities

Formal reviews:

The formal project measurement of success was reporting against an agreed baseline using the formal measurement procedures detailed below.

Baseline:

- Project Objectives - time  quality  cost performance,

- Business Benefits Delivery Plan,

- User Requirements,

- Business Case,

- Measure,

- Project Evaluation/ Lessons Learned Review,

- Close Project,

- Benefits delivery Report,

- Exit business Steering Group control,

- Post Implementation Review,

## 12.12 Conclusions and Summary

The methodology adopted by both organizations has a formal project closedown phase. The review of the new vehicle registration mark project noted the following conclusions in respect of the desirable soft skills and actions required for a collaborative approach to project management:

☐ Set clear objectives and stay focused on them,

- The project managers must actively manage conflict and obtain a resolution,

☐ Set the boundaries for the playing field and allow people the creative freedom to work as a team within the boundaries but don't let ideology take precedence over the success of the project,

☐ Establish an open and honest relationship between both parties and communicate the risks involved to both parties,

☐ Have frequent direct communications both informal and formal. Start out with and maintain a non-confrontational behavioural style,

☐ Build on mutual trust and respect and create an environment of healthy questioning,

- Have joint plans and ensure that risks are actively managed. Allow appropriate notice and lead time for critical tasks,

☐ Allow mistakes to happen - learn from them and move on. The motto 'from a few small failures come greater successes' applies

☐ Use 'active listening' techniques as part of project management style.

# 13. THE PROJECT SCORE CARD QUESTIONNAIRE

## 13.1 The Score Card.

This questionnaire is based on practical experience, gained from a large number of projects in the IT industry. It should be used throughout the project lifecycle.

| Topic Area | Value | True? (Y/N) | Points | Topic Area | Value | True? Y/N) |
|---|---|---|---|---|---|---|
| 1 USER PARTICIPATION | 17.5 | | | 6 PROJECT PLANNING | 10 | |
| Is there a clear focus on user involvement throughout project? | | | 0 | Detailed plans exist for project with clear visibility to user? | | 0 |
| Does the project have representative users? | | | 0 | Project has schedule of small, regular, and attainable milestones? | | 0 |
| Is there a strong working relationship with the user? | | | 0 | Monitoring carried out against plan & communicated to users regularly? | | 0 |
| Have all potential stakeholders been identified and engaged? | | | 0 | Are timely actions being taken against deviations from the plan? | | 0 |
| Project team & customer have agreed | | | 0 | Is project management data being | | 0 |

| expectations for project? | | | collected and used effectively? | | |
|---|---|---|---|---|---|
| | | 0 | | | 0 |
| **2 REQUIREMENTS MANAGEMENT** | **17.5** | | **7 RISK MANAGEMENT** | **5** | |
| Is the project scope clearly defined, agreed, and reviewed regularly? | | 0 | Up to date risk register logging all issues, assumptions, risks reviewed regularly? | | 0 |
| Clear, prioritised, & agreed written document of project requirements reviewed regularly? | | 0 | Prioritised risks according to potential timeliness and impact? | | 0 |
| Can prototypes be used to verify project requirements? | | 0 | Regular reviews of risk register involving whole project team and user? | | 0 |
| Mechanism for changes to requirements in place and actively being used? | | 0 | Project has escalation pathway for dealing with potential risks? | | 0 |
| Trace-ability of reqts against project deliverables? | | 0 | Project has written plans for acting on potential & actual | | 0 |

| | | | | | |
|---|---|---|---|---|---|
| | | | risks? | | |
| | | 0 | | | 0 |
| 3 COMMUNICATION | 15 | | 8 TECHNICAL ENVIRONMENT | 5 | |
| Are regular status reviews held for whole project team? | | 0 | Project team have technical knowledge required to complete project? | | 0 |
| Customer relationship maintained through regular communication? | | 0 | Project manager has ability and time to manage project? | | 0 |
| Documented communication plan exists and is lived? | | 0 | Project has access to correct development tools & tool knowledge? | | 0 |
| Effective internal & external reporting procedures? | | 0 | Is training programme in place to ensure required skills provided? | | 0 |
| Policy for team members to provide feedback? | | 0 | Supporting resources provided to ensure successful completion? | | 0 |
| | | 0 | | | 0 |
| 4 BUSINESS ORIENTATION | 12.5 | | 9 QUALITY MANAGEMENT | 5 | |

| | | | | | |
|---|---|---|---|---|---|
| Do the project objectives align with the business strategy? | | 0 | Does agreed and documented quality plan exist and being lived? | | 0 |
| Does project have business case that details business benefits? | | 0 | Do practices & standards followed adhere to quality plan? | | 0 |
| Can the business benefit be measured? | | 0 | Are non-functional quality attributes required covered in quality plan? | | 0 |
| Does project team understand business domain? | | 0 | Are deviations from standards & concessions documented? | | 0 |
| Representation from all key areas of business impacted? | | 0 | Are internal work product reviews taking place? | | 0 |
| | | 0 | | | 0 |
| 5 PROJECT TEAM | 10 | | | | |
| Committed executive sponsor with necessary authority? | | 0 | | | |
| Shared common vision and common objectives? | | 0 | | | |
| Is there a sense of joint | | 0 | | | |

| responsibility for ownership? | | | | | | |
|---|---|---|---|---|---|---|
| Does the project team have defined roles? | | 0 | | | | |
| Does everyone in the team understand and perform their roles? | | 0 | | | | |

| | | | | | | |
|---|---|---|---|---|---|---|
| *OVERALL PROJECT STATUS:* | | Green: 80-100 | | | | |
| | | Amber: 61-79.5 | | | | |
| Version: 1.0A Version Date: 22Aug 15 | | Red: 0-60.5 | TOTAL PROJECT SUCCESS POTENTIAL (0-100) | | | |

## 13.2 KEY AREAS AND SELF-ASSESSMENT FORM

| Key Area | Workshop Module | Functional Skills Workshop | Self-assessment Pre-Workshop ABCD (A=Excellent D=Poor) | Self-assessment During Workshop ABCD (A=Excellent D=Poor) | Self-assessment End of Coaching ABCD (A=Excellent D=Poor) |
|---|---|---|---|---|---|
| 1. Integration Management | 1.1 Components | • Goals/performance measurements<br>• Project variances (Earned Value, Service Performance Indicators) | | | |
| | 1.2 Integrated Change Management | • Change control plan<br>• Assess ongoing project status<br>• Interpret and handle variances as part of project control (analysis) | | | |
| 2. Scope Management | 2.1 Scope Control | • Analyze impact on project scope, time, budget, staff etc.<br>• Analyze scope change within existing contract or contract addendum<br>• Facilitate change control board where applicable | | | |

| Key Area | Workshop Module | Functional Skills Workshop | Self-assessment Pre-Workshop ABCD (A=Excellent D=Poor) | Self-assessment During Workshop ABCD (A=Excellent D=Poor) | Self-assessment End of Coaching ABCD (A=Excellent D=Poor) |
|---|---|---|---|---|---|
| | | • Assess alternatives of scope change outcomes <br> • Decide how to escalate / involve | | | |
| | 2.2 Estimating | • Define and manage the appropriate estimating process usage | | | |
| | 2.3 Require ments & project scope | • Agree & manage requirements, expectations, opportunities (acceptance criteria and sign-offs) | | | |
| 3. Time Manage ment | 3.1 Schedule | • Create and maintain appropriate multiple schedules <br> • Define appropriate measurements <br> • Identify and consider stakeholder needs <br> • Balance the need for details against | | | |

| Key Area | Workshop Module | Functional Skills Workshop | Self-assessment Pre-Workshop ABCD <br> (A=Excellent D=Poor) | Self-assessment During Workshop ABCD <br> (A=Excellent D=Poor) | Self-assessment End of Coaching ABCD <br> (A=Excellent D=Poor) |
|---|---|---|---|---|---|
| | | comprehensiveness (detailed versus summarized schedule) <br> • How to handle the dynamics of changing baselines also according to performance measurement | | | |
| | 3.2 Time Recording | • Establish time tracking as an element of the project outlook <br> • Perceive time recording as part of an overall reporting process <br> • Manage planned effort vs. actual effort, <br> • Define and control appropriate thresholds <br> • Create and interpret reports <br> • Define required project (administrative) profiles | | | |
| | 3.3 WBS (ES) | • Define business model | | | |

| Key Area | Workshop Module | Functional Skills Workshop | Self-assessment Pre-Workshop ABCD (A=Excellent D=Poor) | Self-assessment During Workshop ABCD (A=Excellent D=Poor) | Self-assessment End of Coaching ABCD (A=Excellent D=Poor) |
|---|---|---|---|---|---|
| | | constraints.<br>• **Balance Schedule with regard to project schedule control and project time/financial control** | | | |
| 4. Cost Management | 4.1 Cost Model | • **Create appropriate project cost model.(considering inventory costing)**<br>• **Manage Cost Centres (cross charging)**<br>• **Handle purchasing and billing procedures** | | | |
| | 4.2 P&L Outlook | • **Manage cost variances and adapt outlooks**<br>• **Define performance measures**<br>• **Handle expense reporting** | | | |
| | 4.3 Budget | • **Define/manage project budgets within the business model context** | | | |

| Key Area | Workshop Module | Functional Skills Workshop | Self-assessment Pre-Workshop ABCD (A=Excellent D=Poor) | Self-assessment During Workshop ABCD (A=Excellent D=Poor) | Self-assessment End of Coaching ABCD (A=Excellent D=Poor) |
|---|---|---|---|---|---|
| 5. Quality Management | 5.1 Quality Plan | • Manage the Quality Plan(s) and the QA processes<br>• Define/implement actions for optimizing project performance | | | |
| | 5.2 Configuration Management. Plan | • Manage Plan(s); usage of results to optimize project and/or perform corrective actions of the overall project change control | | | |
| | 5.3 Project Standards and Procedures | • Control effectiveness of project standards and procedures | | | |
| 6. Human Resource Management | 6.1 Managing Resources | • Assess required skills and compile resource estimates<br>• Utilize the Process for staffing the project<br>• Utilize community & individual networks to identify required skills | | | |

| Key Area | Workshop Module | Functional Skills Workshop | Self-assessment Pre-Workshop ABCD (A=Excellent D=Poor) | Self-assessment During Workshop ABCD (A=Excellent D=Poor) | Self-assessment End of Coaching ABCD (A=Excellent D=Poor) |
|---|---|---|---|---|---|
| | | • **Create skills inventory and resource estimates**<br>• **Maintain Resource Plans** | | | |
| | **6.2 Project team Development** | • **Create & maintain project team Development Plans**<br>• **Organize appropriate team building activities** | | | |
| **7. Communications Management** | **7.1 Communication Plan** | • **Define overall communication plan and strategy**<br>• **Oversee relevant project internal & external communication**<br>• **Decide about on 'marketing" activities** | | | |
| | **7.2 Inter-group Coordination, Affected Groups** | • **Co-ordinate deliverables from external groups**<br>• **Manage and escalate issues and risks** | | | |

| Key Area | Workshop Module | Functional Skills Workshop | Self-assessment Pre-Workshop ABCD (A=Excellent D=Poor) | Self-assessment During Workshop ABCD (A=Excellent D=Poor) | Self-assessment End of Coaching ABCD (A=Excellent D=Poor) |
|---|---|---|---|---|---|
| | | • Push/pull necessary information on time<br>• Manage virtual teams (what works / what does not work)<br>• Differentiate between appropriate working practices in a multi-vendor environment | | | |
| | 7.3 Reporting (Status, Dashboard, Variance Analysis, Trend Analysis, Earned Value) | • Manage project status for overall project (understand that project control does not simply equal project reporting)<br>• Establish guidelines, summaries / filters or sub-reports when appropriate<br>• Understands the effects of reporting. | | | |
| | 7.4 Project | • Market outside immediate area (comfort | | | |

| Key Area | Workshop Module | Functional Skills Workshop | Self-assessment Pre-Workshop ABCD (A=Excellent D=Poor) | Self-assessment During Workshop ABCD (A=Excellent D=Poor) | Self-assessment End of Coaching ABCD (A=Excellent D=Poor) |
|---|---|---|---|---|---|
| | Public Relations | zone) | | | |
| 8. Risk Management | 8.1 ABCD Risk Management | • Define appropriate risk process (prompting of management action) <br> • Decide on the level of customer involvement on project processes <br> • Decide on central versus de-central maintenance of risks | | | |
| 9. Procurement Management | 9.1 Contract | • Structure and manage contract deliverables <br> • Issue and manage contracts within matrix organizations and with suppliers <br> • Consider impact of contract type for projects <br> • Negotiate contracts with | | | |

| Key Area | Workshop Module | Functional Skills Workshop | Self-assessment Pre-Workshop ABCD (A=Excellent D=Poor) | Self-assessment During Workshop ABCD (A=Excellent D=Poor) | Self-assessment End of Coaching ABCD (A=Excellent D=Poor) |
|---|---|---|---|---|---|
| | | third party supplier/contractor | | | |
| | 9.2 Purchase Scenario | • Manage purchase orders with third party | | | |
| 10. Other | 10.1 Strategic Value Selling | • Assess the process deliverables relative to project (input, deliverables, case scenario) | | | |
| | 10.2 Organizational Model and PPM Community | • Consider shared practices from the Project Community | | | |
| | 10.3 Business Context | • Consider existing business plan impact on project | | | |

# 14. WORKSHOP ACTIVITIES

## 14.1 Workshop Abstract

| Goals: | 6. Train and intensify Project Management disciplines based on requirements of target audience. |
|---|---|
| | 7. Compile and review of Project Management deliverables, based on a Case Study using processes and templates. |
| | 8. Knowledge assimilation of Corporate standards (PM2, GSMS, ABCD) and their links to industry standards (PM). |
| | 9. Facilitated exchange of participants' experiences. |
| | 10. Counselling and coaching of participants on project related and IDP related activities through (a max 4 week) tutoring phase. |
| Prerequisites: | 5. Individual Development Plan (IDP) must be in place. |
| | 6. Knowledge and experience about Project Management methods. |
| | 7. Knowledge and experience about methods overview & navigation. |
| | 8. Participants should be engaged in leading project/s most of their time. |

| Content: | 1. Pre-workshop Arrangements for Participants: |
|---|---|
| | • Reading and understanding the Abstract of the Case Study supplied, |
| | • Comprehension of the PM Key Areas, their modules and narrative, |
| | • Filling in of the PM Key Areas self-assessment form, |
| | • Understanding the Case Study Score Card and its components, |
| | • Reading the Workshop Agenda and drafting additional needs, if necessary. |
| | 2. Subjects included in the Workshop: |
| | • Discussion based on the Pre-workshop activities, |
| | • Benefits of Project Management, |
| | • Project Management functions and the interfacing of standards, |
| | • Functional skills for Programme/Project Managers, |
| | • The impact of Project Management, |
| | • Processes, templates usage and PM best practices, |
| | • Group exercise based on Case Study, |

| | |
|---|---|
| | • Discussion on Post-workshop coaching.<br><br>3. Focus on Project Management disciplines (workshop modules) according to the Case Study work:<br><br>For every workshop module there will be:<br><br>• Brief discussion of theory.<br><br>• Practical (case study based) exercises in groups.<br><br>• Facilitated discussion of deliverables and exchange of experience<br><br>4. Organising the coaching phase, which follows the workshop:<br><br>• Define the participant's individual goals.<br><br>• Agree individual development activities for the four weeks of coaching. |
| Methods: | 4. Pre-workshop:<br><br>Abstract of Case Study, PM Key Areas self-assessment form, Case Study Score Card and workshop agenda.<br><br>5. Interactive workshop:<br><br>Consisting of different interfacing modules and based on a generic Case Study with integrated exercises, followed by tutoring. PM Key Areas self-assessment form for |

|  | workshop, Score Card for Case Study assessment.<br><br>6. Post-workshop:<br><br>PM Key Areas self-assessment form, coaching agreement for main points raised and overall schedule for mentoring. |
|---|---|
| Duration: | Three days workshop, followed by four weeks of tutoring phase. |
| Developed by: | Department responsible for Service Excellence |
| Costs: | Local Workshop Deliverer and participant's effort and expenses. |

## 14.2 TRAINING SCHEDULE

| Time Table | Topics | Method and Goals | Material/s | Who |
|---|---|---|---|---|
| *1.3*　*DAY ONE*<br><br>1.4　Session starts at 10.30<br><br>1.5　5 minutes | Opening of WS and welcoming of participants. | Introduction by WS deliverer | None | WS deliverer |
| 12 participants x 2 minutes each = 24 minutes<br>*10.30 – 11.00* | Participants getting acquainted. | Salutations and introductory activities | None | Participants |
| 60 minutes<br><br>*11.00 – 12.00* | • Objectives of WS and the PPFGN Curriculum<br><br>• WS ground rules<br><br>• Agenda and WS | • Presentation of topics to group,<br><br>• Consensus on WS rules,<br><br>• Presentation of agenda, | Presentation displayed via beamer<br><br><br>Pin-boards, | WS deliverer |

| Time Table | Topics | Method and Goals | Material/s | Who |
|---|---|---|---|---|
| | structure<br><br>•Scope of WS | • Presentation of topics which can be addressed in WS,<br><br>• Address problems. (Individual problems will be discussed in depth during coaching session),<br><br>• Mapping of individual issues to WS issues,<br><br>• Placement.<br><br>• Charts displayed in room during WS,<br><br>• Agenda displayed in room to mark progress.<br><br>• Verbal explanation of WS | pins, pens, cards and labels<br><br>Usual facilitation material & accessories<br><br>Confidentiality | |

| Time Table | Topics | Method and Goals | Material/s | Who |
|---|---|---|---|---|
| **45 minutes** <br> *12.00 – 12.45* | **BREAK for LUNCH** | | | |
| 60 minutes <br><br> *12.45 - 13.45* | Participants' expectations & goals. <br><br> Facilitated discussion of completed pre-activities. | Facilitate discussion of WS group. <br><br> The following questions and points are used as a guidance for the participants: <br><br> • What do you want to get out of this WS? <br><br> • List your 3 main goals. <br><br> • In which area would you like to enhance you knowledge? <br><br> • List areas where you would like to be supported during coaching period. | Have the points listed on flipchart, whiteboard, or displayed via beamer <br><br> Make use of the PM Key Ares, as an auxiliary aid to the discussion <br><br> Utilise the Score Card, as an example on how to review the WS case study and projects in | WS deliverer steering the discussion. <br><br> WS participants to discuss. |

| Time Table | Topics | Method and Goals | Material/s | Who |
|---|---|---|---|---|
| | | • List most critical issue in a current project.  • What prevents your project from being successful?  • What will make your project successful? | general | |
| 15 minutes  _13.45 – 14.00_ | Sum up of major points requiring further attention | List the most important thing/s, lesson/s learned and tool/s to be shared among candidates. | Flipcharts/white board | Candidates |
| 60 minutes  _14.00 – 15.00_ | Integrated Methodologies.  Introduction to Project Management | Project Management, Change, and Risk Management and Structured Methodologies.  Integration of Methodologies.  Project Management principles. | Displayed via beamer. | WS Deliverer. |

| Time Table | Topics | Method and Goals | Material/s | Who |
|---|---|---|---|---|
| **15 minutes** *15.00 –15.15* | **Mid-afternoon break** | | | |
| 60 minutes *15.15 – 16.15* | **Mapping of participants' individual expectations (pre-activities) to WS issues (matrix).** | Grouping of top 3 expectations and/or issues on Pin-board. Participants to write issues, problems, observations down on cards and pin them on pin-board in the respective area of matrix: • Identification of Issues, • Writing issues and problems on cards. • Grouping of cards into predefined headings, based on the PMI key areas. • Reviewing of cards with group, | Group activity. Pin-board with prepared matrix. | Participants' classification |

| Time Table | Topics | Method and Goals | Material/s | Who |
|---|---|---|---|---|
| | | • Clarification where applicable,<br><br>• Identification of duplicated points and re-group were applicable. | | |
| 60 minutes<br><br>*16.15 – 17.15* | Case Study Review<br><br>Part 1<br><br>Create collection of the issues and problems, which the participants identified in the case study during the pre-WS preparation.<br><br>State what individual issues/problems will be addressed | Case Study Requirements<br><br>Participants to write issues, problems, observations down on cards and pin them on pin-board under the respective heading:<br><br>Identification of Issue.<br><br>Writing issues & problems on | Top level Requirements Catalogue, based on an existing operational system.<br><br>Pin board<br><br>Defined headings to group issues. | WS deliver/ facilitator<br><br>WS participants' input of findings |

| Time Table | Topics | Method and Goals | Material/s | Who |
|---|---|---|---|---|
| | Create Case Study Plans, | cards.<br><br>Teams to Plan the Case Study and the expected development.<br><br>Discuss and agree Plans. | | |
| | Group candidates into teams, | Grouping of cards into predefined headings based on the PM key areas. | | |
| | Identify Leader, Analysts, User/s and other roles, within each team. | Review of cards with group:<br>• Clarify where applicable,<br>• Eliminate doubles,<br>• Re-group were applicable. | | |
| DAY TWO<br>15 minutes<br>*09:00–0 9:15* | Recap of day 1 | Presentation | Displayed via beamer with reference to wall material | WS Deliverer |
| 60 minutes<br><br>*09.15 – 10.15* | The PM Key Areas | Review the personal issues and problems the participants provided during 'Participants | Pin board<br><br>Defined | WS deliverer |

| Time Table | Topics | Method and Goals | Material/s | Who |
|---|---|---|---|---|
| | **Integration of PMI Key Areas and the Case Study**<br><br>**Case Study Review**<br><br>**Part 2**<br><br>Add individual project issues etc. to collection of case study issues. | expectations & goals' topic.<br><br>Add them to the collection of issues & problems identified in the case study where applicable.<br><br>Doing so, will address some of the identified issues and problems.<br><br>Solutions and recommendations will follow, during the workgroup session. | headings to group issues. | |
| **15 minutes**<br>*10.15 – 10.30* | **Mid-morning Break** | | | |
| **60 minutes**<br><br>*10.30 – 11.30* | **Case Study Review**<br><br>Re-group candidates into workgroups of Leader, Analysts, User/s and other roles. | At beginning of WS each participant is provided with a role, which states a problem or activity, based on WS module, functional skills, and any other PM key area. | Number of areas are distributed equally to the number of participants | WS deliverer to ask every participant at beginning of WS to agree on roles and activities. |

127

| Time Table | Topics | Method and Goals | Material/s | Who |
|---|---|---|---|---|
| | | The content of the envelope to be grouped with the persons that have the same area stated on their cards. | | |
| 60 minutes<br><br>*11.30 – 12.30* | Case Study Review<br><br>Plan session<br><br>Each workgroup to be presented with one problem area, the associated issues and problems | Each Workgroup to identify:<br><br>• Root cause/underlying problem, Recommendation on how to fix it, Define solution.<br>• Input: issues collection<br><br>• Process: Participants use flipchart of slides to collect their findings.<br><br>• Media is used to present findings and recommendations to large groups | • Define time allowed for exercise<br><br>• Separate groups within meeting room<br><br>• Flipchart paper, pens<br><br>• Allocate timescales for presentations, for each | Individual workgroups<br><br>WS deliverer to interact with groups to track progress and help where appropriate |

| Time Table | Topics | Method and Goals | Material/s | Who |
|---|---|---|---|---|
| | | • Output: recommendations to solve issues – of case study, and for the raised issues of the individuals | group<br><br>• Define template of points to be addressed during presentation, based on root cause, alternative way to resolve issue and recommendation. | |
| 45 minutes<br>*12:30 –13.15* | BREAK for LUNCH | | | |
| 60 minutes<br><br>*13.15 – 14.15* | Case Study Review<br><br>Presentations of Workgroup results | Root causes and resolutions proposal to be presented by workgroups, | Charts / slides as prepared by | Workgroups |

| Time Table | Topics | Method and Goals | Material/s | Who |
|---|---|---|---|---|
| | | Discussion of proposed solutions, Group feedback. WS deliver provides additional feedback on group findings after the initial discussion. Add personal experience/best practice advice. | | |
| 60 minutes <br> *14.15-15.15* | Results of workgroups | Presentation and discussion | Group activity | Participants |
| 15 minutes <br> *15.15 – 15.30* | **Mid-afternoon Break** | | | |
| 60 minutes <br><br> *15.30 – 16.30* | Project Managers' Pre-selected Exercise | Points pre-selected by participants, based on the Project Score Card and as summarised on Cobb's Paradox diagram. | Participants to write their goals and objectives. | Teams |

| Time Table | Topics | Method and Goals | Material/s | Who |
|---|---|---|---|---|
| | Goal setting | Participants to team up<br><br>Participants to display principles of teamwork<br><br>Participants' listing of individual goals for the next 4 weeks.<br><br>Participants to list the top 3<br><br>things they want to achieve<br><br>within the next 4 weeks.<br><br>Participants to define the<br><br>support they will require. | Should be copied to team member/s, as a reference.<br><br>One copy to WS deliverer/coach, listing the goals the participant would like to achieve. | |

| Time Table | Topics | Method and Goals | Material/s | Who |
|---|---|---|---|---|
| | | Goals identified for the coaching period. | | |
| 60 minutes<br><br>*16.30 – 17.30* | Goal setting discussion.<br><br>Share goals, if possible.<br><br>Progress Review | Participants should be<br><br>encouraged to share goals.<br><br><br>Statement as to whether the WS assisted in achieving the goals. | Goal documentation of the participants | Participants |
| DAY THREE 15 minutes<br>*09:00 – 09:15* | Recap of day 2 | Presentation | Displayed via beamer with reference to wall material | WS Deliverer |

| Time Table | Topics | Method and Goals | Material/s | Who |
|---|---|---|---|---|
| 60 minutes<br><br>*09.15 – 10.15* | Summing up of results<br><br><br><br><br>Tutoring Process and future activities organising.<br><br>Agree on individual schedules. | WS Deliverer to sum up exercise findings.<br><br>Groups of participants to select Speaker to represent their findings.<br><br>Presentation by group leaders to those present<br><br>Explain what happens after the WS<br><br>Naming of coach and subsequent steps for mentoring.<br><br>Explain confidentiality of conversations between coach and participants. | Presentation | Participants/ group leaders<br><br><br><br><br><br>Facilitator |
| 15 minutes<br>*10.15 – 10.30* | Mid-morning Break | | | |

| Time Table | Topics | Method and Goals | Material/s | Who |
|---|---|---|---|---|
| 60 minutes<br>*10.30 – 11.30* | Tutoring Process and future activities organising. | Explain what happens after the WS | Talk | WS deliverer |
| 60 minutes<br><br>*11.30 – 12.30* | Agree on individual schedules. | Naming of coach and subsequent steps for mentoring.<br><br>Explain confidentiality of conversations between coach and participants. | Talk<br><br>One to One discussion | Participants<br><br>WS deliverer |
| 45 minutes<br>*12:30 – 13.15* | BREAK for LUNCH | | | |
| 60 minutes<br><br>*13.15 – 14.15* | Case Study, ENTITY MODEL/S<br><br>Assessment of Entity Model/s, Check that Plans have been met,<br><br>Skills Evaluation | Participants' Presentations of Entity Model/s.<br><br>Ascertain that PLANNED objectives have been met.<br><br>Offer additional support, if any specific topics were not fulfilled. | Participants' presentations of Entity Models.<br><br>Discussion<br><br>Counselling | Participants<br><br>Participants<br><br>Participants and Facilitator. |

| Time Table | Topics | Method and Goals | Material/s | Who |
|---|---|---|---|---|
| 15 minutes <br> *14.15 – 14.30* | Mid-afternoon Break | | | |
| 60 minutes <br> *14.30 – 15.30* | Course Evaluation by Participants. <br><br> Conclusion of Workshop. | Participants' feedback and comments regarding the WS. | Written Individual and Personal method of Participant's own overall Workshop Evaluation. (No standard forms will be provided.) <br><br> Round table discussion | Participants |

# 15. THE WORKSHOP

- WORKSHOP STRUCTURE

- THE AGENDA

## PRE-WORKSHOP ACTIVITIES

- THE BUSINESS MODEL

- INTERFACING OF METHODOLOGIES

- WORKSHOP FUNCTIONAL SKILLS

- PROJECT MANAGEMENT FUNCTIONS

- BENEFITS OF PROJECT MANAGEMENT

- THE WORKSHOP CASE STUDY

## POST-WORKSHOP COACHING

- PRE-WORKSHOP ACTIVITIES

- PROGRAMME MANAGEMENT KEY AREAS

- THE SELF-ASSESSMENT FORM

- THE CASE STUDY

- THE SCORE CARD

- THE WORKSHOP

- CONCEPTS AND MEASURES

## THE MANAGEMENT OF KEY AREAS

- INTEGRATION

- SCOPE

- TIME

- COST

- QUALITY

- HUMAN RESOURCE

- COMMUNICATION

- RISK

- PROCUREMENT

INTERFACING

- METHODOLOGIES

- PROGRAMME MANAGEMENT

- RISK MANAGEMENT

WORKSHOP FUNCTIONAL SKILLS

- FILLING THE GAP

- PROJECT MANAGEMENT OVERVIEW

- THE FUNDAMENTALS

- STANDARDS

MANAGEMENT FUNCTIONS

- INTRODUCTION TO MANAGEMENT FUNCTIONS

- INFORMATION SYSTEMS DEVELOPMENT CYCLE

- PROJECT MANAGEMENT AND PLANNING TECHNIQUE

- MANAGING PROJECTS

- SOLUTIONS

PROJECT MANAGEMENT AND THE POST-WORKSHOP COACHING AND MENTORING

PROGRAMME/PROJECT MANAGEMENT (PM), A PROFESSION

- POST-WORKSHOP COACHING AND MENTORING

- THE INTERPERSONAL SKILLS OF THE COACH

THE BENEFITS OF PROJECT MANAGEMENT

Actual users have attributed the summarised main benefits listed below to Project Management.

1. PROVIDES THE BASIS FOR CONTROLLING THE IMPLEMENTATION OF STRATEGIC BUSINESS PLANS.

2. PROMOTES THE BUSINESS VIEW FOR THE JUSTIFICATION OF PROJECTS AND PROVIDES MECHANISMS FOR ENSURING THEIR ONGOING VIABILITY AND BUSINESS INTEGRITY.

3. THE ORGANISATION STRUCTURE ENCOURAGES USER AND BUSINESS PARTICIPATION AT ALL LEVELS AND CAN BE TAILORED TO ANY TYPE, SIZE AND COMPLEXITY OF PROJECT.

4. SEPARATES AND CLEARLY IDENTIFIES AND DEFINES, THE ROLES AND RESPONSIBILITIES IN PROJECT MANAGEMENT.

5. THE STAGE CONCEPT PROVIDES THE BASIS FOR CONSCIOUS AND CONTINUOUS MANAGEMENT CONTROL.

6. CONCENTRATES ON THE REAL GOALS OF THE PROJECT, THROUGH THE PRODUCTS, TO ENSURE A COMMON UNDERSTANDING ABOUT WHAT IS BEING PRODUCED. THIS PRODUCT

ORIENTATION ALSO ENABLES BETTER ESTIMATING, PLANNING AND CONTROL.

7. THE PLANNING AND CONTROL MECHANISMS ARE TAILORED AND STRUCTURED TO ONE ANOTHER.

8. QUALITY IS PLANNED, CONTROLLED AND ASSURED FROM THE OUTSET OF THE PROJECT.

9. PROVIDES AN EXCELLENT VEHICLE FOR ENCOURAGING THE RIGHT PEOPLE TO MAKE THE RIGHT DECISION AT THE RIGHT TIME.

10. CONFRONTS THE MANAGEMENT OF RISK AND UNCERTAINTY BY ASKING QUESTIONS AND FORCING ISSUES

INTO THE OPEN. DEALING WITH ISSUES CAN REDUCE PROJECT COSTS BEFORE THEY BECOME PROBLEMS.

11. SIMPLIFIES PAPERWORK BY CONCENTRATING ON ESSENTIAL DOCUMENTATION AND THE PROVISION OF SIMPLE BUT EFFECTIVE REPORTING PROCEDURES.

# 16. USER PARTICIPATION

| 1. User Participation |
|---|
| The project has a responsibility to involve the user from conception through to delivery and beyond. This helps reduce the opportunity for misunderstandings, assists in the management of expectations, and promotes a collaborative approach to development. |
| Not only must the project involve users, but it must ensure that the users are representative of the whole user population. Different departments have different needs as do different job functions within those departments. |
| There must be a healthy and co-operative relationship between the user and the development team. This can be encouraged through two way communications on a regular basis, both formally and informally. |
| Whilst user involvement is critical, there will be other parties with a vested interest in the outcome of a project. These parties need to be identified and kept in touch with project progress. |
| By maintaining open lines of communication with the user the project can be spared the shock of unpleasant surprises when milestones are missed, and expensive and unnecessary rework can be avoided early on. |

## 2. Requirements Management

One of the quickest ways for a project to spiral out of control is failure to agree and document the scope of the project and its business objectives.

Requirements must be documented and prioritised with the agreement of the user and the development team. Requirements must be accurate, realistic, and unambiguous and stated at the right level of detail as demanded by the stage of the project.

Functional or usability prototypes are an ideal method for verifying requirements and are relatively inexpensive to build. If prototypes are used, their use must be carefully managed along with user expectations. A prototype is not a complete system.

Change Control mechanisms and a Change Control Board with both user and project representatives must be in place before requirements changes can be made.

All requirements should be traceable from the original objectives through to the project deliverables. Traceability must be bi-directional. This ensures that all customer requirements have been met.

## 3. Communication

The whole project team should be kept informed about the progress and status of the whole project throughout the development lifecycle. This encourages teamwork and ownership in the project as a whole.

Unless the communication line between the user and the project team remains open it is impossible for the team to manage the expectations of the user, and the team will lose valuable feedback from the user.

A clear communications plan assures both user and project team of their commitment to communicate with each other in a timely and regular manner.

Project managers need to ensure that correct and accurate information is flowing through to all affected parties in a timely fashion. Informed team members are more effective than uninformed ones.

There must be an active policy to allow any member of the project team to escalate project issues and concerns either in person or anonymously to the appropriate level of management.

## 4. Business Orientation

Projects are started to fulfil specific business needs which address the overall strategic aims of the business. Embarking on projects which are beyond the organisation's experience are likely to be inherently risky.

IT projects are there to serve specific business needs and a documented business case within a value

| |
|---|
| proposition is essential elements for project success. |
| Appropriate measures must be in place to monitor the commercial benefit to the business. The metrics must be defined and a baseline set down to monitor against. |
| It is essential that at least some members of the IT project team have exposure to the problem domain to ensure that project staff and customers understand a common language |
| IT projects often have to serve diverse business needs simultaneously and all impacted business areas must be represented as stakeholders in the project. |

| 5. Project Team |
|---|
| Projects need an individual, who has recognised standing within the organisation, to act as the project champion and to assist in removing obstacles that impact on the project's chance of success. |
| There must be a common vision and understanding of the project objectives. Hidden agendas lead to conflict between members of the team and jeopardise the project as a whole |
| All members of the team need to feel that they have shared ownership of the project. This instills a sense of responsibility and commitment, and an inherent desire to perform at the highest level. |
| The project team needs clear definitions of roles and responsibilities ; e.g. Risk Manager, Configuration |

| Manager etc. |
| --- |
| Team members must have clear understanding of their own responsibilities but also other team member's responsibilities and the interfaces through which they must communicate. |

| 6. Project Planning |
| --- |
| Projects need clear and visible schedules for their delivery commitments which are agreed with the customer, senior management, and the project team. Regular and early delivery reduces the risk of misunderstandings. |
| A project that commits to unrealistic and unattainable schedules will fail. Small and regular milestones help to keep a project on track and maintain customer confidence. |
| It is not in the interest of the customer or the project to conceal problems and regular customer facing progress reports must be produced. |
| If a project is facing problems in keeping to its plans, actions must be assigned to individuals on the project team and escalated to the appropriate level of management at the earliest opportunity. |
| The project must ensure that project metrics are maintained to assist in planning and estimation both for the project itself and future projects. |

| 7. Risk Management |
|---|
| A risk register is a dynamic tool used to document everything that has a potential negative effect on the project. The account recommends the used of the ABCD method of risk analysis. |
| All items recorded in the risk register must be prioritised and estimates made of size, likelihood and timing of their impact on the project. |
| The risk register must be maintained throughout the life of the project and must be visible to all members of the project team. Ownership of the risk register will usually reside with the project manager or a nominated risk manager. |
| The project must ensure that plans are in place to prevent risks happening or to reduce their effect if they cannot be prevented. Risk plans must be regularly reviewed and executed in a timely manner if necessary. |
| It is understood that project teams will not always have the authority to execute their risk plans, and must ensure that appropriate lines of escalation are in place to take action. It is not usually good policy to transfer risk to other parties. |

## 8. Technical Environment

A certain amount of project work can be learnt "on the job", but a project team must have a core number of people with the requisite technical knowledge to ensure that the team functions efficiently at the outset.

A project is likely to fail unless it has committed IT and User project managers adequate time and ability to fulfil their roles.

Project team members must be provided with the appropriate development environment and the right tools to enable them to function at an optimum level, e.g. Configuration Management tools,

Training requirements must be identified early and incorporated into the project schedule. Training plans should be timed so that skills can be deployed as soon as possible after they are learnt.

Projects need supporting facilities to function correctly, e.g. real estate, administrative functions, hardware, etc. Resource acquisition must be executed as the project requirements demands.

## 9. Quality Management

The "Quality Plan" is a single document or set of documents that describes the measures that the project team will undertake to ensure that a satisfactory level of quality is maintained.

| |
|---|
| The project team must document its standards and practices in the Quality plan, and must ensure that these are being adhered to. Failure to observe documented practice may lead to withdrawal of ISO 9000 certification. |
| For software development projects it is vital to ensure that service oriented (non-functional) quality attributes such as performance, reliability are documented in the quality plan |
| It is recognised that projects may have to deviate from the QMS for specific reasons, but it is important that any deviations and their associated concessions are documented in the quality plan. |
| The Account is mandated to put all deliverable work products through peer review to maximise their value to the customer and to provide a learning experience for members of the project team. |

# 17. PROGRAMME CHANGES

## 17.1 SCOPE WITHIN THE PROGRAMME

Once the Project has started, a project change management team manages all changes. If there are any changes, a proposed solution is constructed and sent to all relevant teams (internal and often external to the project) for impact assessment. If the change has limited impact and can be funded from existing authorised funds, the Project/Programme board or director can authorise the change. It is up to the Project/Programme board to decide that the change needs to be escalated, either as funding is required, or because of the impact it may have on other projects/programmes.

If the change is approved, it would be implemented and if the change is rejected, the change notification/details will reflect the reason it is rejected. This cycle of changes to Project/Programme scope is continued for each change that is required, until the implementation is complete.

## 17.2 OPTIONS

The purpose of this section is to identify and outline the main options available for Change Management. A recommended option will be developed further into a plan for how the proposed solution will be implemented. Each solution for managing change across the account can be characterised under the following four categories:

- Governance: The method in which changes are approved. It is possible that a single change may require budget approval. It is usually Governance that causes the biggest delays in any process and not obtaining necessary sign off can be disastrous, hence getting the hierarchy and escalation processes right is essential.

- Culture: The way in which people work together. The ideal culture for changes to be managed effectively is a true partnership. Hence each option must strive to drive the teams to work together better.

- Process: The steps people take to manage change. This is a purist point of view, of what activities take place in order to manage a change from a concept to an implemented product. This would include standards for forms and communication guidelines.

- Tool: Whether there is one tool to support a single process, or a number of tools that interface well with each other, the right tool/s has to be developed to meet the established Process requirements.

## 17.3 UNCERTAIN EVENTS

A change is an uncertain event, which may have an adverse effect on the project's objectives. Using the Change Management methodology should be very effective in the quest for identifying changes throughout the project lifecycle.

Remember, the Change Management methodology is:

- Forward looking, investigating problems and how to deal with threats,
- A tool enabling communication, getting people at all levels to talk to each other and to interact,
- A no blame team culture, bringing concerns into the open where actions can be taken and plans put in place, in order to stop a change occurring.

# 17.4 MANAGEMENT QUALITIES REQUIRED

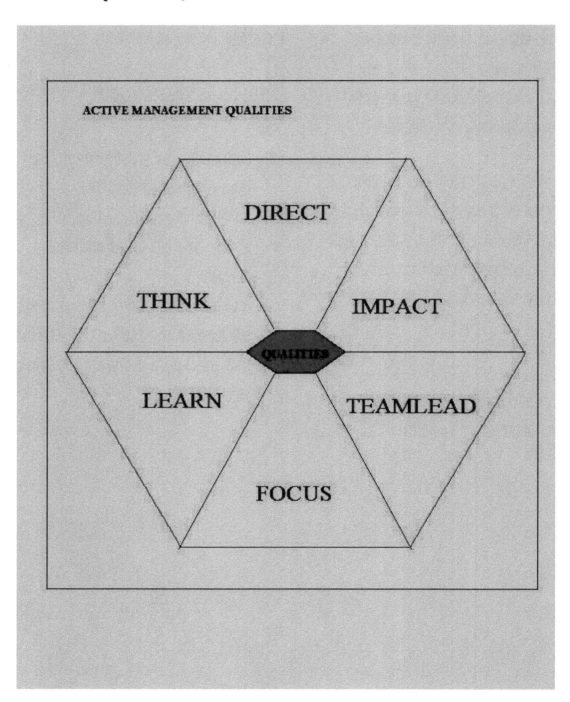

# 18. PROJECT SCORING

## 18.1 SCORE GRAPH

**A scoring card graph can easily be produced on a spreadsheet and it could look something like this:**

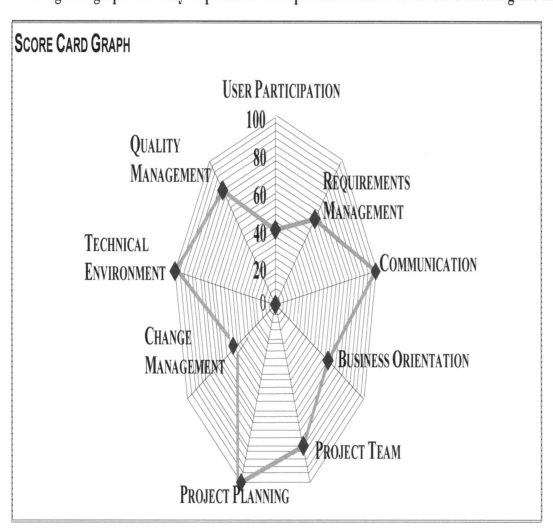

## 18.2 SCORING POINTS

### 1: USER PARTICIPATION                                  17.5

Is there a clear focus on user involvement throughout project?

Does the project have representative users?

Is there a strong working relationship with the user?

Have all potential stakeholders been identified and engaged?

Project team & customer have agreed expectations for project?

### 2: REQUIREMENTS MANAGEMENT

Is the project scope clearly defined, agreed, and reviewed regularly?

Clear, prioritized, & agreed written document of project requirements reviewed regularly?

*Andreas Sofroniou*

Can prototypes be used to verify project requirements?

Mechanism for changes to requirements in place and actively
being used?

Traceability of requirements against project deliverables?

## 3: COMMUNICATION                                    15

Are regular status reviews held for whole project team?

Customer relationship maintained through regular communication?

Documented communication plan exists and is lived?

Effective internal & external reporting procedures?

Policy for team members to provide feedback?

## 4: BUSINESS ORIENTATION                             12.5

Do the project objectives align with the business strategy?

Does project have business case that details business benefits?

Can the business benefit be measured?

Does project team understand business domain?

Representation from all key areas of business impacted?

## 5: PROJECT TEAM                                    10

Committed executive sponsor with necessary authority?

Shared common vision and common objectives?

Is there a sense of joint responsibility for ownership?

Does the project team have defined roles?

Does everyone in the team understand and perform their roles?

1
0

## 6: PROJECT PLANNING

Detailed plans exist for project with clear visibility to user?

Project has schedule of small, regular, and attainable milestones?

Monitoring carried out against plan & communicated to users regularly?

Are timely actions being taken against deviations from the plan?

Is project management data being collected and used effectively?

## 7: CHANGE MANAGEMENT                              7.5

Up to date risk register logging all issues, assumptions, risks
   reviewed regularly?

Prioritized risks according to potential timeliness and impact?

Regular reviews of risk register involving whole project team and user?

Project has escalation pathway for dealing with potential risks?

Project has written plans for acting on potential & actual risks?

## 8: TECHNICAL ENVIRONMENT

Project team has technical knowledge required to complete project?

Project manager has ability and time to manage project?

Project has access to correct development tools & tool knowledge?

Is training program in place to ensure required skills provided?

Supporting resources provided to ensure successful completion?

## 9: QUALITY MANAGEMENT

Does agreed and documented quality plan exist and being lived?

Do practices & standards followed adhere to quality plan?

Is non-functional quality attributes required covered in quality plan?

Are deviations from standards & concessions documented?

Are internal work product reviews taking place?

*OVERALL PROJECT STATUS:*

Green:

80-100

Amber:

61-79.5

Red:

0-60.5

## 18.3 SCORING EXPLANATION

| 1. USER PARTICIPATION |
|---|
| The project has a responsibility to involve the user from conception through to delivery and beyond. This helps reduce the opportunity for misunderstandings, assists in the management of expectations, and promotes a collaborative approach to development. |
| Not only must the project involve users, but it must ensure that the users are representative of the whole user population. Different departments have different needs as do different job functions within those departments. |
| There must be a healthy and co-operative relationship between the user and the development team. This can be encouraged through two way communications on a regular basis, both formally and informally. |
| Whilst user involvement is critical, there will be other parties with a vested interest in the outcome of a project. These parties need to be identified and kept in touch with project progress. |
| By maintaining open lines of communication with the user the project can be spared the |

shock of unpleasant surprises when milestones are missed, and expensive and unnecessary rework can be avoided early on.

## 2. REQUIREMENTS MANAGEMENT

One of the quickest ways for a project to spiral out of control is failure to agree and document the scope of the project and its business objectives.

Requirements must be documented and prioritized with the agreement of the user and the development team. Requirements must be accurate, realistic, and unambiguous. Also, stated at the right level of detail as demanded by the stage of the project.

Functional or usability prototypes are an ideal method for verifying requirements and are relatively inexpensive to build. If prototypes are used, their use must be carefully managed along with user expectations. A prototype is not a complete system.

Change Control mechanisms and a Change Control Board with both user and project representatives must be in place before requirements changes can be made.

All requirements should be traceable from the original objectives through to the project deliverables. Traceability must be bi-directional. This ensures that all customer requirements have been met.

## 3. COMMUNICATION

The whole project team should be kept informed about the progress and status of the whole project throughout the development lifecycle. This encourages teamwork and ownership in the project as a whole.

Unless the communication line between the user and the project team remains open it is impossible for the team to manage the expectations of the user, and the team will lose valuable feedback from the user.

A clear communications plan assures both user and project team of their commitment to communicate with each other in a timely and regular manner.

Project managers need to ensure that correct and accurate information is flowing through to all affected parties in a timely fashion. Informed team members are more effective than uninformed ones.

There must be an active policy to allow any member of the project team to escalate project issues and concerns either in person or anonymously to the appropriate level of management.

## 4. BUSINESS ORIENTATION

Projects are started to fulfil specific business needs which address the overall strategic aims of the business. Embarking on projects which are beyond the organization's experience is likely to be inherently risky.

IT projects are there to serve specific business needs and a documented business case within a value proposition is essential elements for project success.

Appropriate measures must be in place to monitor the commercial benefit to the business. The metrics must be defined and a baseline set down to monitor against.

It is essential that at least some members of the IT project team have exposure to the problem domain to ensure that project staff and customers understand a common language

IT projects often have to serve diverse business needs simultaneously and all impacted business areas must be represented as stakeholders in the project.

## 5. PROJECT TEAM

Projects need an individual, who has recognized standing within the organization, to act as the project champion and to assist in removing obstacles that impact on the project's chance of success.

There must be a common vision and understanding of the project objectives. Hidden agendas lead to conflict between members of the team and jeopardize the project as a whole

All members of the team need to feel that they have shared ownership of the project. This instills a sense of responsibility and commitment, and an inherent desire to perform at the highest level.

The project team needs clear definitions of roles and responsibilities ; e.g. Risk Manager, Configuration Manager etc.

Team members must have clear understanding of their own responsibilities but also other team member's responsibilities and the interfaces through which they must communicate.

## 6. PROJECT PLANNING

Projects need clear and visible schedules for their delivery commitments which are agreed with the customer, senior management, and the project team. Regular and early delivery reduces the risk of misunderstandings.

A project that commits to unrealistic and unattainable schedules will fail. Small and regular milestones help to keep a project on track and maintain customer confidence.

It is not in the interest of the customer or the project to conceal problems and regular customer facing progress reports must be produced.

If a project is facing problems in keeping to its plans, actions must be assigned to individuals on the project team and escalated to the appropriate level of management at the earliest opportunity.

The project must ensure that project metrics are maintained to assist in planning and estimation both for the project itself and future projects.

## 7. CHANGE MANAGEMENT

A risk register is a dynamic tool used to document everything that has a potential negative effect on the project. The account recommends the used of the ABCD method of risk analysis.

All items recorded in the risk register must be prioritized and estimates made of size, likelihood and timing of their impact on the project.

The risk register must be maintained throughout the life of the project and must be visible to all members of the project team. Ownership of the risk register will usually reside with the project manager or a nominated risk manager.

The project must ensure that plans are in place to prevent risks happening or to reduce their effect if they cannot be prevented. Risk plans must be regularly reviewed and executed in a timely manner if necessary.

It is understood that project teams will not always have the authority to execute their risk plans, and must ensure that appropriate lines of escalation are in place to take action. It is not usually good policy to transfer risk to other parties.

## 8. TECHNICAL ENVIRONMENT

A certain amount of project work can be learnt "on the job", but a project team must have a core number of people with the requisite technical knowledge to ensure that the team functions efficiently at the outset.

A project is likely to fail unless it has committed IT and User project manager's adequate time and ability to fulfill their roles.

Project team members must be provided with the appropriate development environment and the right tools to enable them to function at an optimum level, e.g. Configuration Management tools,

Training requirements must be identified early and incorporated into the project schedule. Training plans should be timed so that skills can be deployed as soon as possible after they are learnt.

Projects need supporting facilities to function correctly, e.g. real estate, administrative functions, hardware, etc. Resource acquisition must be executed as the project requirements demands.

## 9. QUALITY MANAGEMENT

The "Quality Plan" is a single document or set of documents that describes the measures that the project team will undertake to ensure that a satisfactory level of quality is maintained.

The project team must document its standards and practices in the Quality plan, and must ensure that these are being adhered to. Failure to observe documented practice may lead to withdrawal of ISO 9000 certification.

For software development projects it is vital to ensure that service oriented (non-functional) quality attributes such as performance, reliability are documented in the quality plan

It is recognized that projects may have to deviate from the QMS for specific reasons, but it is important that any deviations and their associated concessions are documented in the quality plan.

The Account is mandated to put all deliverable work products through peer review to maximize their value to the customer and to provide a learning experience for members of the project team.

INDEX OF CHAPTERS IN ALPHABETICAL SEQUENCE

# BIBLIOGRAPHY

ALL BOOKS LISTED BELOW ARE WRITTEN BY THE AUTHOR, ANDREAS SOFRONIOU.

## INFORMATION TECHNOLOGY AND MANAGEMENT

1.  I.T. RISK MANAGEMENT, ISBN: 978-1-4467-5653-9
2.  SYSTEMS ENGINEERING, ISBN: 978-1-4477-7553-9
3.  BUSINESS INFORMATION SYSTEMS, CONCEPTS AND EXAMPLES, ISBN: 978-1-4092-7338-7
4.  A GUIDE TO INFORMATION TECHNOLOGY, ISBN: 978-1-4092-7608-1
5.  CHANGE MANAGEMENT IN I.T., ISBN: 978-1-4092-7712-5
6.  FRONT-END DESIGN AND DEVELOPMENT FOR SYSTEMS APPLICATIONS, ISBN: 978-1-4092-7588-6
7.  I.T RISK MANAGEMENT, ISBN: 978-1-4092-7488-9
8.  I.T. RISK MANAGEMENT – 2011 EDITION, ISBN: 978-1-4467- 5653-9
9.  THE SIMPLIFIED PROCEDURES FOR I.T. PROJECTS DEVELOPMENT, ISBN: 978-1-4092-7562-6
10. THE SIGMA METHODOLOGY FOR RISK MANAGEMENT IN SYSTEMS DEVELOPMENT, ISBN: 978-1-4092-7690-6
11. TRADING ON THE INTERNET IN THE YEAR 2000 AND BEYOND, ISBN: 978-1-4092- 7577
12. STRUCTURED SYSTEMS METHODOLOGY, ISBN: 978-1-4477-6610-0
13. INFORMATION TECHNOLOGY LOGICAL ANALYSIS, ISBN: 978-1-4717-1688-1
14. I.T. RISKS LOGICAL ANALYSIS, ISBN: 978-1-4717-1957-8
15. I.T. CHANGES LOGICAL ANALYSIS, ISBN: 978-1-4717-2288-2
16. LOGICAL ANALYSIS OF SYSTEMS, RISKS , CHANGES, ISBN: 978-1-4717-2294-3
17. COMPUTING, A PRÉCIS ON SYSTEMS, SOFTWARE AND HARDWARE, ISBN: 978-1-2910-5102-5
18. MANAGE THAT I.T. PROJECT, ISBN: 978-1-4717-5304-6
19. CHANGE MANAGEMENT, ISBN: 978-1-4457-6114-5
20. THE MANAGEMENT OF COMMERCIAL COMPUTING, ISBN: 978-1-4092-7550-3
21. PROGRAMME MANAGEMENT WORKSHOP, ISBN: 978-1-4092-7583-1
22. MANAGEMENT OF I.T. CHANGES, RISKS, WORKSHOPS, EPISTEMOLOGY, ISBN: 978-1-84753-147-6
23. THE PHILOSOPHICAL CONCEPTS OF MANAGEMENT THROUGH THE AGES, ISBN: 978-1-4092- 7554-1
24. THE MANAGEMENT OF PROJECTS, SYSTEMS, INTERNET, AND RISKS, ISBN: 978-1-4092- 7464-3

25. HOW TO CONSTRUCT YOUR RESUMÊ, ISBN: 978-1-4092-7383-7

26. DEFINE THAT SYSTEM, ISBN: 978-1-291-15094-0

27. INFORMATION TECHNOLOGY WORKSHOP, ISBN: 978-1-291-16440-4

28. CHANGE MANAGEMENT IN SYSTEMS, ISBN: 978-1-4457-1099-0

29. SYSTEMS MANAGEMENT, ISBN: 978-1-4710-4907-1

30. TECHNOLOGY, A STUDY OF MECHANICAL ARTS AND APPLIED SCIENCES, ISBN: 978-1-291-58550-6

31. EXPERT SYSTEMS, KNOWLEDGE ENGINEERING FOR HUMAN REPLICATION, ISBN: 978-1-291- 59509-3

32. ARTIFICIAL INTELLIGENCE AND INFORMATION TECHNOLOGY, ISBN: 978-1-291- 60445-0

33. PROJECT MANAGEMENT PROCEDURES FOR SYSTEMS DEVELOPMENT, ISBN: 978-0-952-72531-2

34. SURFING THE INTERNET, THEN, NOW, LATER. ISBN: 978-1--291-77653-9

35. ANALYTICAL DIAGRAMS FOR I.T. SYSTEMS, ISBN: 978-1-326-05786-2

36. INTEGRATION OF INFORMATION TECHNOLOGY, ISBN: 978-1-312-84303-1

37. TRAINING FOR CHANGES IN I.T. ISBN: 978-1-326-14325-1

38. WORKSHOP FOR PROJECTS MANAGEMENT, ISBN: 978-1-326-16162-0

## MEDICINE AND PSYCHOLOGY

39. MEDICAL ETHICS THROUGH THE AGES, ISBN: 978-1-4092- 7468-1

40. MEDICAL ETHICS, FROM HIPPOCRATES TO THE 21ST CENTURY ISBN: 978-1-4457-1203-1

41. THE MISINTERPRETATION OF SIGMUND FREUD, ISBN: 978-1-4467-1659-5

42. JUNG'S PSYCHOTHERAPY: THE PSYCHOLOGICAL & MYTHOLOGICAL METHODS, ISBN: 978-1-4477-4740-6

43. FREUDIAN ANALYSIS & JUNGIAN SYNTHESIS, ISBN: 978-1-4477-5996-6

44. ADLER'S INDIVIDUAL PSYCHOLOGY AND RELATED METHODS, ISBN: 978-1-291-85951-5

45. ADLERIAN INDIVIDUALISM , JUNGIAN SYNTHESIS, FREUDIAN ANALYSIS, ISBN: 978-1-291-85937-9

46. PSYCHOTHERAPY, CONCEPTS OF TREATMENT, ISBN: 978-1-291-50178-0

47. PSYCHOLOGY, CONCEPTS OF BEHAVIOUR, ISBN: 978-1-291-47573-9

48. PHILOSOPHY FOR HUMAN BEHAVIOUR, ISBN: 978-1-291-12707-2

49. SEX, AN EXPLORATION OF SEXUALITY, EROS AND LOVE, ISBN: 978-1-291-56931-5

50. PSYCHOLOGY FROM CONCEPTION TO SENILITY, ISBN: 978-1-4092-7218-2

51. PSYCHOLOGY OF CHILD CULTURE, ISBN: 978-1-4092-7619-7

52. JOYFUL PARENTING, ISBN: 0 9527956 1 2

53. THE GUIDE TO A JOYFUL PARENTING, ISBN: 0 952 7956 1 2

54. THERAPEUTIC PHILOSOPHY FOR THE INDIVIDUAL AND THE STATE, ISBN: 978-1-4092-7586-2

55. PHILOSOPHIC COUNSELLING FOR PEOPLE AND THEIR GOVERNMENTS, ISBN: 978-1-4092-7400-1

## PHILOSOPHY AND POLITICS

56. MORAL PHILOSOPHY, FROM SOCRATES TO THE 21ST AEON, ISBN: 978-1-4457-4618-0

57. MORAL PHILOSOPHY, FROM HIPPOCRATES TO THE 21ST AEON, ISBN: 978-1-84753-463-7

58. MORAL PHILOSOPHY, THE ETHICAL APPROACH THROUGH THE AGES, ISBN: 978-1-4092-7703-3

59. MORAL PHILOSOPHY, ISBN: 978-1-4478-5037-3

60. 2011 POLITICS, ORGANISATIONS, PSYCHOANALYSIS, POETRY, ISBN: 978-1-4467-2741-6

61. PLATO'S EPISTEMOLOGY, ISBN: 978-1-4716-6584-4

62. ARISTOTLE'S AETIOLOGY, ISBN: 978-1-4716-7861-5

63. *MARXISM, SOCIALISM & COMMUNISM, ISBN: 978-1-4716-8236-0*

64. *MACHIAVELLI'S POLITICS & RELEVANT PHILOSOPHICAL CONCEPTS, ISBN: 978-1-4716-8629-0*

65. BRITISH PHILOSOPHERS, 16TH TO 18TH CENTURY, ISBN: 978-1-4717-1072-8

66. ROUSSEAU ON WILL AND MORALITY, ISBN: 978-1-4717-1070-4

67. EPISTEMOLOGY, ISBN: 978-1- 978-1-326-11380-3

68. HEGEL ON IDEALISM, KNOWLEDGE & REALITY, ISBN: 978-1-4717-0954-8

## SOCIAL SCIENCES AND PHILOLOGY

69. PHILOLOGY, CONCEPTS OF EUROPEAN LITERATURE, ISBN: 978-1-291-49148-7

70. THREE MILLENNIA OF HELLENIC PHILOLOGY, ISBN: 978-1-291-49799-1

71. CYPRUS, PERMANENT DEPRIVATION OF FREEDOM, ISBN: 978-1-291-50833-8

72. SOCIOLOGY, CONCEPTS OF GROUP BEHAVIOUR, ISBN: 978-1-291-51888-7

73. SOCIAL SCIENCES, CONCEPTS OF BRANCHES AND RELATIONSHIPS ISBN: 978-1-291-52321-8

74. CONCEPTS OF SOCIAL SCIENTISTS AND GREAT THINKERS, ISBN: 978-1-291-53786-4

## FICTION AND POETRY

75. THE TOWERING MISFEASANCE, ISBN: 978-1-4241-3652-0

76. DANCES IN THE MOUNTAINS – THE BEAUTY AND BRUTALITY, ISBN: 978-1-4092-7674-6

77. YUSUF'S ODYSSEY, ISBN: 978-1-291-33902-4

78. WILD AND FREE, ISBN: 978-1-4452-0747-6

79. HATCHED FREE, ISBN: 978-1-291-37668-5

80. THROUGH PRICKLY SHRUBS, ISBN: 978-1-4092-7439-1

81. BLOOMIN' SLUMS, ISBN: 978-1-291-37662-3

82. SPEEDBALL, ISBN: 978-1-4092-0521-0

83. SPIRALLING ADVERSARIES, ISBN: 978-1-291-35449-2

84. EXULTATION, ISBN: 978-1-4092-7483-4

85. FREAKY LANDS, ISBN: 978-1-4092-7603-6

86. SOFRONIOU COLLECTION OF FICTION BOOKS, ISBN: 978-1-326-07629-0

87. MAN AND HIS MULE, ISBN: 978-1-291-27090-7

88. LITTLE HUT BY THE SEA, ISBN: 978-1-4478-4066-4

89. THE SAME RIVER TWICE, ISBN: 978-1-4457-1576-6

90. THE CANE HILL EFFECT, ISBN: 978-1-4452-7636-6

91. WINDS OF CHANGE, ISBN: 978-1-4452-4036-7

92. A TOWN CALLED MORPHOU, ISBN: 978-1-4092-7611-1

93. EXPERIENCE MY BEFRIENDED IDEAL, ISBN: 978-1-4092-7463-6

94. CHIRP AND CHAT (POEMS FOR ALL), ISBN: 978-1-291-75055-3

95. POETIC NATTERING, ISBN: 978-1-291-75603-6

www.ingramcontent.com/pod-product-compliance
Lightning Source LLC
Chambersburg PA
CBHW081226050326
40689CB00016B/3696